Jerry Hordinney

GERMAN SHEPHERD TRAINING

The Ultimate Guide

First edition

This book was professionally typeset on Reedsy
Find out more at reedsy.com

Contents

    1.

        1.

        2.

        3.

    2.

        1.

        2.

        3.

        4.

        5.

    3.

        1.

        2.

        3.

        4.

    4.

        1.

        2.

        3.

        4.

    5.

        1.

Preface

The German Shepherd is a well-liked dog breed known for its intelligence, perseverance, and adaptability. Due to their exceptional working abilities, they are frequently utilized as police and military canines and in search and rescue operations. However, German Shepherds make excellent family pets if their owners are willing to put in the time and effort to properly train and care for them.

A German Shepherd can be challenging to train, but it can also be rewarding. A well-trained German Shepherd can be a family member's companion and protector as well as a joy to be around. However, training a German Shepherd involves more than just teaching it basic commands; Knowing how they behave, what they want, and how to communicate effectively with them are necessary.

We will give you an exhaustive outline of how to prepare your German Shepherd from puppyhood to adulthood in this extreme manual for German Shepherd preparing. We will discuss everything from basic obedience commands to advanced training techniques. We'll also talk about important subjects like nutrition and health, grooming, and how to fix common behavioral issues.

This guide will give you the information and tools you need to raise a happy, sturdy, and polite German Shepherd, whether you're a first-time dog owner or an experienced trainer. Therefore, let's get started on the process of teaching your trustworthy and intelligent companion!

German Shepherds are renowned for their high levels of energy and need for mental stimulation. If they don't get enough exercise and training, they might become destructive and bored. In order to give them a way to express their intelligence and energy, proper training and socialization are necessary.

One of the greatest challenges in training is the strong will of the German Shepherd. They are an independent breed that can sometimes be stubborn. With patience, consistency, and positive reinforcement, you can train your German Shepherd to become a well-behaved and obedient companion.

Socialization is just as important as training for German Shepherds. They may be wary of new people and situations because of their protective nature. Your German Shepherd will become more tolerant of people and other animals if you socialize them with them from a young age, reducing the risk of hostility and fear-based behavior.

This guide will cover positive reinforcement training, clicker training, and other methods. We will also provide guidance on how to deal with typical behavioral issues like chewing, jumping, and barking. We will likewise discuss explicit preparation techniques for cutting edge errands like spryness, insurance, and search and salvage.

Whether you want to train your German Shepherd for competitions, as a working dog, or as a family pet, this guide will equip you with the knowledge and skills you need. With the right training and socialization, your German Shepherd can become a reliable and well-behaved companion for many years to come.

Another important part of training a German Shepherd is making sure they get enough food and are healthy. German Shepherds need regular exercise and a well-balanced diet to stay healthy because they are a large breed. We'll discuss the best food varieties for your German Shepherd, the amount to take care of them, and how to set up a taking care of timetable that works for yourself as well as your way of life.

In addition to food, we will discuss German Shepherds' exercise requirements and how to provide them with the appropriate amount of physical activity. We'll talk about how physical and mental health benefits from exercise, as well as how to make exercise enjoyable for your German Shepherd.

We will also demonstrate how to bathe, brush, and trim your German Shepherd's nails. Proper grooming is important for keeping them clean and healthy, and it can strengthen your relationship with your German Shepherd.

It requires investment, persistence, and obligation to prepare a German Shepherd, yet the advantages of having a polite and reliable buddy merit the work. After reading this book, you will have the knowledge and skills you need to properly train and care for your German Shepherd. You will actually want to make major areas of strength for a with your German Shepherd and participate in a happy and satisfying relationship for quite a long time into the future by following the methods and procedures illustrated in this aid.

Why German Shepherds make great pets

Understandably, German Shepherds are an extremely well known canine variety. Due to their adaptability, intelligence, and loyalty, they make excellent family pets for those who are willing to put in the time and effort to properly train and care for them.

German Shepherds are excellent pets due to their intelligence. Because they can be taught a wide range of commands and tasks, they are ideal for a wide range of jobs and activities. Due to their exceptional work ethic, German Shepherds are frequently employed as police and military canines as well as in search and rescue operations. However, dogs also make excellent family pets if their owners enjoy training and exercising them.

Another reason German Shepherds make excellent pets is their loyalty. They are a breed that forms strong bonds with their owners and protects their families fiercely. Due to their reputation for recognizing danger and willingness to protect their family, German Shepherds make excellent watchdogs. They are excellent pets for families with young children due to their unwavering loyalty and self-control.

German Shepherds are also extremely adaptable pets. They can live in a variety of environments and thrive in both urban and rural settings. They are a variety that appreciates actual work, causing them ideal for families who to appreciate swimming, running, and climbing in nature. They enjoy spending time with their owners inside and make excellent indoor pets.

In addition to their intelligence, loyalty, and adaptability, German Shepherds are renowned for their affectionate nature. They are a variety that likes to invest energy with their proprietors and can be exceptionally cherishing and tender toward their relatives. Because of their hospitable nature, they make excellent pets for people looking for a reliable and devoted companion.

Last but not least, German Shepherds are a breed that can stay with you and love you for a long time. They are famous because they can live anywhere from 9 to 13 years, depending on their health and genetics. German Shepherds can provide their owners with numerous long stretches of affection, devotion, and friendship with genuine care and preparation.

In conclusion, German Shepherds are ideal pets due to their intelligence, loyalty, adaptability, affectionate nature, and long lifespans. They are a breed that requires proper training and care, but for those who are willing to put in the effort, they can provide companionship and joy for many years

In spite of their ubiquity as pets, German Shepherds are not appropriate for all people. They're a big, active breed that needs a lot of exercise and mental stimulation. If you live in a small apartment or don't have time to exercise and train your German Shepherd, this breed might not be right for you.

Hip dysplasia and degenerative myelopathy are two additional health issues that can affect German Shepherds. Exploring the variety and finding a legitimate reproducer who has done whatever it takes to guarantee the wellbeing and nonappearance of hereditary problems of their doggies are fundamental.

Additionally, German Shepherds require socialization and training. They are a variety that should be prepared early and frequently to keep away from issues like hostility and nervousness. Your German Shepherd will be more accepting of other people and animals if he has been socialized.

Remember that having a German Shepherd comes with a lot of responsibility. They require a significant amount of time, attention, and resources to ensure their happiness and health. In any case, owning a German Shepherd has endless benefits for those who put in the effort.

German Shepherds are a remarkable breed of dog that make loyal and adored pets. Because of their intelligence, adaptability, and love, they can provide their owners with years of companionship and happiness. If you want a German Shepherd for your family, do your research and find a reputable breeder. With the right care, training, and attention, your German Shepherd can be a wonderful addition to your family and a lifetime companion.

One of the best ways to keep your German Shepherd happy and healthy is to give him or her a lot of physical activity and mental stimulation. Because they are a working breed, German Shepherds require regular exercise to maintain their intellectual vigor and good physical condition. Lack of exercise can lead to behavioral issues like aggression, destructiveness, and anxiety.

You can get your German Shepherd moving by swimming, playing tug-of-war or fetch, and taking him or her on long walks or runs. They also enjoy taking part in activities like nose work, training for obedience, and training for agility. They get exercise and mental stimulation from these activities, which is important for their overall health.

To keep their wellbeing, German Shepherds need to practice and eat well. They must be fed a well-balanced diet that is appropriate for their age, size, and activity level. For their general wellbeing and prosperity, top notch canine food with protein, solid fats, and important nutrients and minerals is fundamental.

German Shepherds require customary veterinary consideration too. They must be regularly examined and vaccinated in order to maintain their health. Additionally, they require routine dental care to prevent tartar buildup and tooth decay.

Another essential aspect of owning a German Shepherd is socialization. Since they are a variety that can be defensive and regional, socialization quite early in life is fundamental. Socialization incorporates introducing them to different people, animals, and conditions to help them with becoming pleasant and certain about different conditions.

For those who are willing to put in the time and effort, German Shepherds make excellent pets when properly cared for. They are a breed that is devoted and affectionate and can give their owners years of companionship and happiness. However, it is essential to keep in mind that maintaining their happiness and health requires a significant amount of time, attention, and resources. Do your research before purchasing a German Shepherd for your family and get ready to give them the love and attention they deserve.

What to expect from this guide

Whether you have recently adopted a German Shepherd or are considering getting one, this guide is an invaluable resource that will provide you with the information you need to properly care for your pet. The guide's goal is to teach you everything you need to know about the German Shepherd breed and the particular requirements it has.

The guide will provide you with in-depth information on training, exercise, nutrition, and health care. We'll go over everything you need to know to make sure your German Shepherd is happy, healthy, and respectful.

Additionally, owners of German Shepherds will receive practical advice on common issues like aggression, separation anxiety, and destructive behavior. We will give you strategies and procedures for dealing with these problems in a positive and practical way.

In addition, this guide contains a wealth of helpful information from seasoned German Shepherd trainers and owners. In order to build a lasting relationship with your pet, you'll learn how to cultivate areas of strength and gain important experiences throughout the range.

In general, this guide is a comprehensive and useful resource that will help you take the best care of your German Shepherd. Whether you've had a German shepherd for a short time or a long time, this guide will provide you with the information and support you need to ensure that your pet is content, healthy, and thriving.

In addition, you will gain a better understanding of the significance of early training and socialization for your German Shepherd with the help of this guide. German Shepherds, a variety known for its high insight and dynamic nature, require organized preparing to assist them with growing beneficial routines and ways of behaving. We'll show you effective training techniques that will help you build a strong foundation for your pet's development.

You will also learn how important it is to give your German Shepherd a lot of mental and physical stimulation. German Shepherds need a lot of exercise and mental stimulation to stay happy and healthy because they are a working breed. To assist you in avoiding common behavioral issues like boredom and destructive behavior, we will demonstrate how to create a stimulating environment for your pet.

In this guide, we will also discuss the various types of German Shepherd-specific feeding regimens and nutrition. It is fundamental for your pet's general wellbeing and prosperity to take care of them an eating regimen that is even. We'll show you how to select a high-quality dog food and set a feeding schedule that suits your pet's needs.

Last but not least, you'll find helpful tips for keeping your German Shepherd happy and healthy. We'll show you how to regularly groom and clean your pet to keep it clean and comfortable. We'll also talk about common health issues that can affect German Shepherds and give you advice on how to prevent and treat them.

In general, this guide is a comprehensive resource that will help you take the best care of your German Shepherd. If you follow the tips and tricks in this guide, you'll be able to bond deeply with your pet and ensure that they live a long and healthy life.

This guide will also discuss important aspects of German Shepherd behavior like aggression, socialization, and anxiety. Because German Shepherds can be prone to certain behavioral issues if they are not properly socialized, it is essential to begin socializing your puppy as soon as possible. We will demonstrate to you how to socialize your German Shepherd so that they become sociable and well-adjusted adults as adults.

We'll also talk about common German Shepherd traits like aggression and anxiety. Aggression in German Shepherds can be a serious problem if it is not addressed appropriately. We'll show you how to identify warning signs of your pet's aggression and how to handle it constructively and effectively.

Another common problem that German Shepherds may experience is anxiety, especially if they are not given enough mental and physical excitement. We'll show you how to recognize your pet's signs of anxiety and offer suggestions for dealing with it and making it less of a problem.

Finally, advanced German Shepherd training methods will be covered in this guide. As a breed with a high intelligence level, German Shepherds are capable of learning numerous advanced behaviors and tricks. Scent work, tracking, and agility are just a few of the advanced training techniques we will demonstrate to you for your pet.

In general, this guide is an invaluable resource for anyone who wants to provide their German Shepherd with the best possible care. This guide will furnish you with the data and bearing you really want to guarantee that your pet is content, sound, and respectful, whether you are a carefully prepared canine sweetheart or a first-time proprietor.

Understanding your German Shepherd's behavior

Because they are a smart and active breed, German Shepherds require a lot of physical and mental stimulation. The way to furnishing your German Shepherd with the consideration and consideration they expect to flourish is to understand their way of behaving. In this section, we will discuss some of the most significant aspects of German Shepherd behavior.

Understanding the German Shepherd's inherent need to protect their family is one of the most important aspects of their behavior. German Shepherds are excellent watchdogs and family members due to their reputation for loyalty and security. In any case, on the off chance that your pet isn't as expected mingled and prepared, this defensive impulse may likewise appear as animosity.

Socialization is an essential component of German Shepherd behavior, and it ought to begin as soon as possible. The most common method of introducing your pet to a wide range of people, things, and circumstances in a positive and controlled way is through socialization. Your German Shepherd can figure out how to communicate with others in a quiet and well disposed manner and foster great interactive abilities through socialization.

Another important characteristic of German Shepherd behavior is the need for physical activity and mental stimulation. German Shepherds need a lot of physical and mental stimulation to stay happy and healthy because they are a working breed. If your pet doesn't get enough exercise and mental stimulation, they may become bored and destructive. This can cause conduct issues like biting, digging, and yelping excessively.

German Shepherds are also known to be very active and have a lot of energy. If they are not exercised and trained properly, they may become hyperactive. Regular exercise, such as daily walks and playtime, can help your pet shed excess energy while also keeping him or her calm and focused.

In addition to exercising, it's important to give your German Shepherd mental stimulation. Mental stimulation can come from interactive games, puzzle toys, and training sessions. These exercises can assist with keeping your pet's brain sharp and hold that person back from getting exhausted and acting damagingly.

Finally, it's fundamental to grasp that German Shepherds can be leaned to explicit clinical issues, similar to hip dysplasia and lump. Standard veterinary consideration, a solid eating routine, and normal activity are exceptionally significant in light of the fact that these issues can influence your pet's way of behaving and by and large personal satisfaction.

In conclusion, if you want to give your German Shepherd the attention and care they need, it's important to know how they act. You can guarantee that your German Shepherd is content, solid, and respectful by associating it, giving it a lot of activity and mental feeling, and observing their wellbeing and prosperity.

Additionally, it is essential to be aware of some typical issues with the behavior of German Shepherds. One of the most common issues is separation anxiety, which can cause your pet to become overly attached and anxious when you aren't around. This can lead to horrible behavior, unreasonable yelling, and other bad behavior. In order to assist in the prevention of separation anxiety, it is essential to gradually acclimate your pet to being alone, provide them with ample mental stimulation, and provide them with toys to keep them occupied.

Hostility is another behavior problem that can affect German Shepherds, especially if they aren't as social and prepared as expected. Growling, biting, and lunging are all examples of aggressive behaviors that can be displayed. If you notice any signs of aggression in your pet, you must address the problem as soon as possible with the help of a trained trainer or behaviorist.

However, anxiety and fear can also influence German Shepherd behavior. Traumas from the past, a lack of socialization, or genetics can all contribute to these issues. Fear and anxiety can manifest themselves in a number of different ways, including hiding, shaking, and avoiding social situations. To help your pet overcome these obstacles, provide them with plenty of positive reinforcement, a safe and comfortable environment, and, if necessary, professional guidance.

In conclusion, learning to comprehend your German Shepherd's behavior requires time, effort, and a willingness to learn. By being aware of your pet's preferences and requirements, you can provide the care and attention they require to be happy and healthy. With genuine socialization, work out, and setting up, your German

Shepherd can transform into a courteous and treasuring partner long into what's to come.

Understanding your German Shepherd's behavior also requires recognizing their body language and communication cues. German Shepherds, like all dogs, communicate their feelings and intentions through a variety of signals. Learning to read and interpret these signals can help you better understand what your pet is trying to tell you.

German Shepherds typically communicate through nonverbal cues like the following:

- **Tail position:** A tail that is brought down can indicate dread or complacency, whereas a tail that is raised indicates certainty and joy.
- **Ears:** While ears that are flat can indicate fear or aggression, ears that are pricked convey interest and alertness.
- **Eye contact:** A direct eye-to-eye connection can indicate certainty or hostility, whereas avoiding eye-to-eye contact can indicate dread or acceptance.
- **Body posture:**A relaxed, loose posture indicates happiness and contentment, whereas a stiff, tense posture can indicate fear or aggression.

By zeroing in on your German Shepherd's non-verbal correspondence and correspondence signals, you can all the more promptly sort out their prerequisites and sentiments. This can strengthen your bond with your pet and assist you in addressing any challenges or behavioral issues that may arise.

In addition to comprehending their behavior and communication cues, it is essential to provide your German Shepherd with the genuine care and preparation they require to thrive. Included in this are healthy eating, regular exercise, and proper grooming. In addition, it involves teaching them basic commands and introducing them to other pets and people.

Understanding your German Shepherd's behavior is generally one of the most crucial aspects of providing them with the care and attention they require. By being aware of your pet's preferences and requirements, you can foster a strong bond with them and ensure that they   live   a   happy   and   fulfilled   life.

PUPPY TRAINING

Puppy training is an essential component of raising a happy and well-behaved dog. When you adopt a puppy, you not only get a new pet but also take on the responsibility of training them and introducing them to other people so they can become a well-adjusted member of your family.

The first few months of a puppy's life are crucial to their growth and development. During this time, they acquire knowledge of their surroundings, interact with other animals and people, and develop their personalities and behaviors. It is essential to provide your puppy with a safe and nurturing environment in which they can explore and learn in addition to setting boundaries and expectations for their behavior.

Effective puppy training includes teaching your pet the fundamental commands "sit," "stay," and "come," as well as housetraining them to go outside to urinate. In order for them to develop good manners and learn how to behave in social situations, they must also be socialized with other pets and people.

In addition to having many practical benefits, puppy training is a great way to get to know your new pet. During training sessions, one-on-one interaction and positive reinforcement can help your puppy form a lasting bond.

However, training small dogs can also be difficult and time-consuming. It requires perseverance, patience, and an openness to adapting to your puppy's unique needs and learning style. It is essential to approach puppy training with a positive and proactive mindset and to seek professional assistance if you are experiencing difficulties or feeling overwhelmed.

In this guide, we will give you the information and resources you need to train your new puppy well. We'll talk about dealing with common behavioral issues, house training, socialization, and basic obedience training. With the right approach and effort, you can assist your puppy in becoming a family member who is well-behaved and content.

Establishing a positive and profitable preparing environment is an important part of dog training. Positive reinforcement, which can be used to encourage good behavior and deter bad behavior, includes affection, praise, and treats. It tends to be hindering to your relationship with your doggy and be counterproductive to rebuff or reprimand your little dog for making trouble.

Socialization is one more fundamental part of pup preparing. Through socialization, if you expose your puppy to a wide range of people, animals, and environments, he or she will learn to feel at ease and confident in a variety of settings. As a result, behaviors like fear and aggression toward other dogs or strangers can be prevented.

Housetraining is yet another essential aspect of puppy training. This includes teaching your dog to go outside to urinate and preventing accidents inside the house. Consistency, patience, giving your puppy plenty of opportunities to go outside, and rewarding good behavior with treats and praise are the keys to successful house training.

Taking care of common behavior problems like chewing, jumping, and barking is an important part of puppy training. Giving your puppy appropriate toys and redirecting their behavior when necessary can stop destructive chewing and other bad behaviors. Showing your dog important submission commands like "sit" and "remain" can also help stop hopping and woofing.

We will provide you with step-by-step instructions and practical advice on the best way to prepare your new puppy in this guide. Container preparation, rope preparation, and fundamental orders will all be covered. In addition, we'll give you tips on how to deal with common behavioral issues and make training enjoyable and rewarding for your pet.

Typically, puppy training is an important part of raising a happy and composed dog. With the right approach and effort, you can help your puppy become a well-behaved and adored member of your family.

Puppy training is an essential part of owning a dog because it lays the groundwork for a well-mannered and content pet. It is essential to begin preparing as soon as possible because the first few months of a dog's life are crucial for their socialization and learning how to get along with other dogs. This section will discuss the fundamentals of puppy training, including house training, socialization, and basic commands for obedience.

House training, also known as potty training, is one of the first and most important aspects of puppy training. Showing your dog where to go potty and preventing accidents inside the house can help establish positive routines and prevent future behavioral issues. Follow these tips for successful house training:

1. Establish a routine:

Young dogs often need to use the bathroom, especially after eating or sleeping. Establish a routine for taking your dog outside every two to three hours, as well as after meals and time to rest.

2. Reward good behavior:

Give your doggy treats and love when they go outside to assuage themselves. As a result of this positive reinforcement, your puppy will associate going outside to urinate with good things.

3. Supervise your puppy:

When your puppy is not in their crate, keep a close eye on them to prevent accidents inside the house. As soon as you notice your dog beginning to use the bathroom inside, take him or her outside.

4. Use a crate:

Establishing a routine and avoiding house accidents can be accomplished through crate training. Keep your little dog in their box when you can't be there to watch them since pups normally could do without to go potty where they rest.

Socialization To assist your pup with becoming confident and balanced, socialization involves presenting them to different individuals, creatures, and conditions. This is pivotal for staying away from issues with conduct like trepidation, tension, and animosity toward different canines or outsiders. Here are some recommendations for successful socialization:

1. Start early:

Pups have a basic time of socialization between the ages of 3 and 14, so start acquainting them with new things quickly.

2. Use positive reinforcement:

When introducing new experiences to your puppy, reward them with treats and praise to help them associate those new experiences with positive emotions.

3. Be patient:

Because some puppies may initially be hesitant or afraid of new experiences, take your time and don't force them into uncomfortable situations.

4. Socialize with other dogs:

Socialization with other dogs is essential for teaching your puppy good manners and preventing behavioral issues. Take into consideration enrolling your puppy in a kindergarten class or attending puppy playgroups with them.

Fundamental Submission Orders Teaching your puppy the basic commands "sit," "remain," and "come" can help establish positive routines and prevent behavioral issues. The following are some suggestions for teaching your puppy basic commands:

1. Use positive reinforcement:

When your dog exhibits the best behavior, reward them with treats and praise. They can connect positive feelings and acceptable conduct therefore.

2. Keep training sessions short and frequent:

Puppy attention spans are short, so keep training sessions brief and frequent throughout the day.

3. Be patient:

Be patient and don't get annoyed; a few pups might demand more investment to learn orders than others.

4. Be consistent:

Use the same word and hand gesture each time you ask your puppy to do something. This encourages good habits and makes it easier for them to understand what you want.

In conclusion, dog ownership requires puppy training. You can assist with forestalling social issues and raise a blissful, respectful pet by ingraining positive routines from the get-go. Pup preparation entails house training, socialization, and fundamental duty orders, all of which can be accomplished with the right approach, persistence, and consistency.

Another essential component of puppy training is socialization. The process of introducing your puppy to a wide range of people, animals, and environments is known as socialization. This is done to help your puppy develop a confident and well-rounded personality. A puppy that has been socialized well is less likely to be anxious or aggressive as a child.

Introduce your puppy to a variety of people, including children, adults, and the elderly, to begin socializing them. They should also be exposed to cats, other dogs, and, if at all possible, farm animals. It's also important to let your puppy try new things, so take them for walks in the park, to the beach, or to other public locations where they can see and hear new things.

Positive and controlled introductions to new things should be given to your puppy. Over time, increase the number of times they are exposed to various stimuli and constantly praise them for their good behavior. For example, if your puppy is afraid of other dogs, walk them on a leash with a calm, friendly dog at first. Give them treats and acclaim assuming they answer emphatically. Increase the duration and intensity of these interactions gradually until your puppy is comfortable interacting with other dogs.

Another part of puppy training is teaching your puppy basic commands like "sit," "stay," "come," and "heel." These commands establish you as the pack leader and help your puppy comprehend what is expected of them. Using praise and treats as positive reinforcement is the most effective method for training your puppy.

Keeping your puppy's training sessions short and enjoyable is essential. Training sessions should be limited to 10 to 15 minutes and include a lot of positive reinforcement because puppies have short attention spans and are prone to becoming easily distracted. When it comes to dog training, consistency is everything, so make sure that everyone in the family follows the same set of rules and rewards.

As a general rule, pup preparing is a significant piece of raising a German Shepherd who is polite and balanced. You can help your puppy grow into a happy, confident, and devoted adult dog by starting early and using positive feedback methods.

Preparing for your puppy's arrival

Preparing for the arrival of a new German Shepherd is an exciting and crucial step in adopting one. It is essential to ensure that you have everything you need to provide a secure and comfortable home for your new pet.

One of the first things you should think about when getting ready for your puppy's arrival is where they will sleep. A cozy and inviting bed for your puppy to sleep in will be necessary. An excellent option is a crate, which not only provides your puppy with a safe environment but also assists in potty training.

In addition, you must ensure that your puppy has the appropriate supplies. A leash and collar, grooming supplies, water bowls, toys, and food and water bowls are all part of this. It is essential to select high-quality food designed specifically for puppies in order to ensure that they receive the necessary nutrition for growth and development.

Puppy proofing your home is also essential to ensure your puppy's safety. This means getting rid of anything that could be harmful, like toxic plants, wires, chemicals, and other things. In order to keep some parts of your house out, you might also need to install baby gates.

It means a lot to contemplate the progressions to your timetable and lifestyle that accompany getting another doggy. Puppies require a lot of thought and care, including customary potty breaks, break, and educational gatherings. It is fundamental to guarantee that you have the opportunity and energy to give to the prerequisites of your new doggy.

Last but not least, as soon as you return home, take your puppy to the veterinarian. Your puppy's overall health will be assessed by your veterinarian, who will also be able to administer any necessary treatments or vaccinations.

In general, getting ready for your puppy's arrival requires a lot of planning and preparation. By properly preparing your schedule and home, you can help ensure a successful transition for both you and your new pet.

Another important part of getting ready for your puppy's arrival is establishing rules and boundaries. This includes setting boundaries for your puppy's home and setting expectations for his behavior, such as not jumping on furniture or other people.

It is also essential to begin crate training your puppy as soon as possible. This means gradually introducing your puppy to their crate and forming a bond with it. Providing your puppy with a safe place to rest, assisting in potty training, and preventing destructive behavior when you are not home are just a few of the many benefits of crate training.

Another important aspect of getting ready for your puppy is socialization. As part of its socialization, your puppy needs to be exposed to a wide range of people, animals, and environments in a positive and controlled way. This helps your dog become agreeable and upbeat about new situations and can prevent later social issues like fear or animosity.

As you get ready for your puppy's arrival, remember that patience and consistency are essential. The time and effort required to properly train and care for a new puppy are well worth the advantages of having a companion who is content and well-behaved.

You can assist with guaranteeing that your new pet will carry on with a long and satisfied life by finding opportunity to plan for its appearance and establish a strong starting point for preparing and care appropriately.

Having the vital supplies close by is all one more significant piece of preparing for your little dog. This includes things like a box, a bed, water and food bowls, great little dog food, toys, and supplies for cooking.

A high-quality puppy food that is appropriate for your puppy's age and breed is essential. Talk to your veterinarian about the type of food that is best for your puppy, as well as how much and how often to feed it.

It's just as important to mentally and emotionally prepare for your new puppy as it is to buy the necessary things. Because puppies require a significant amount of care, attention, and training, it is essential to be prepared for the responsibility of raising a young dog.

Consider enrolling in a puppy training class and conducting research on puppy training and behavior prior to the arrival of your puppy. These classes can be of great assistance and support in navigating the challenges of raising a young dog.

Patience and understanding are essential as you welcome your new puppy into your home. Puppies are always curious and have a lot of energy. They will always make errors as they learn and grow. By remaining calm, consistent, and encouraging in your interactions with your puppy, you can assist in its development into an adult dog who is content and well-behaved.

House training

House training, also known as potty training or house training, is an essential part of puppy training. In order to prevent accidents and maintain a clean environment, house training teaches your puppy to urinate outside rather than inside.

One of the first steps in house training is to create a routine. This includes taking your puppy for a walk in the morning, after meals and naps, and before bedtime. Consistency is necessary for establishing a routine and teaching your puppy when and where to urinate.

During the course of the house training process, it is also essential to keep a close eye on your puppy. Keep an eye out for signs like sniffing or circling that indicate they need to go outside when they are indoors, and keep them in a small space or on a leash. Right when you notice these signs, speedily take your little guy outside to their relegated potty spot.

Positive reinforcement is an essential part of house training. Give your puppy enthusiastic praise and a small treat when they excrete outside. They continue to engage in the behavior as a result, and they learn that it is advantageous to eliminate outside sources.

Accidents will unavoidably occur during house training; However, patience and avoiding punishment are essential. Instead, simply wipe up any spills to get rid of any odors that might make your dog want to urinate there once more.

Another piece of house planning is assisting your pup with making you when they need mindful of head outside. This can be done by teaching your puppy to ring a bell or to use a specific command to tell them they need to go outside, keeping a consistent routine, and using positive reinforcement.

With patience, consistency, and positive reinforcement, you can teach your puppy to eliminate outside and keep your home clean. Training at home can be challenging. By spreading out a regular work on, managing your pup eagerly, using elevating input, and avoiding discipline, you can help your little canine with developing extraordinary bathroom penchants and become a pleasant person from your loved ones.

You can slowly build your pup's opportunity inside the house as they become more predictable with their washroom schedule. This can be done by gradually increasing the amount of space your puppy can roam in while always keeping an eye on them and looking for signs that they need to go outside.

It is essential to keep in mind that house training can take several weeks or even months to complete and that every puppy learns at their own pace. By practicing patience and consistency in your training, you can be ready for setbacks or accidents along the way.

There are a few additional suggestions and deceptions that can assist with the preparation of the house, in addition to laying out a routine for the day and making use of encouraging feedback. One way to help your puppy control how often they pee is to feed them on a regular basis. Provide your puppy with a consistent spot outside to go potty can help them associate that location with the behavior you want from them.

Some puppies may also benefit from crate training during house training. A crate can provide your puppy with a secure environment when you are unable to supervise them. Teaching them to hold their bladder and wait until they need to go outside can also help with potty training.

In general, house training is an essential component of puppy training because it can assist in maintaining a clean home and preventing accidents. You can show your little dog great restroom propensities and assist them with turning into a polite individual from your family with tolerance, consistency, and encouraging feedback.

Another important part of house training is keeping a close eye on your puppy when they are indoors. This means keeping them in a designated area of the house, such as a playpen or a room made safe for puppies, and watching closely for signs that they need to go outside. A couple of typical signs that a little canine requirements to discard integrate sniffing around, circumnavigating, and crying or woofing.

If you find your puppy excreting indoors, you must immediately take them outside to finish and calmly but firmly interrupt them. Scolding or punishing your puppy can be confusing and counterproductive, so avoid doing so. Instead, concentrate on rewarding your puppy for going outside to relieve himself or herself and gradually reducing the number of accidents as they become more consistent.

Additionally, in order to get rid of any odor and discourage your puppy from using the same spot again, it is essential to thoroughly and immediately clean up any accidents. Cleaners with ammonia in them should be avoided because the smell can actually encourage dogs to urinate there once more. All things being equal, utilize an enzymatic cleaner planned explicitly for pet stains.

As they become more consistent with their bathroom habits, you can gradually give your puppy more freedom inside and begin moving them to off-leash outdoor potty breaks. Notwithstanding, to keep away from relapse and mishaps, it is crucial for keep implementing beneficial routines and sticking to a reliable daily schedule.

In general, house training is an essential component of puppy training. Patience, perseverance, and praise are required. With the right approach, you can assist your puppy in developing good toileting habits and prepare them for success as an obedient adult dog.

Basic obedience commands

Basic commands for obedience must be learned by all dogs, including German Shepherds. As well as giving an establishment to further developed preparing and guaranteeing your canine's security and appropriate conduct in different circumstances, they help with laying out clear correspondence among you and your canine.

The basic submission commands "sit," "remain," "down," "come," and "heel" are the most well-known. Each of these commands can be taught using positive reinforcement strategies, and each serves a distinct purpose.

Your dog will learn to sit on command if you teach it the command "Sit," which is frequently one of the first commands taught. This can be achieved by utilizing a treat or toy to cajole your canine into a sitting position, step by step eliminating the draw, and adding the verbal order "sit." Your canine will discover that sitting when you say "sit" is an acceptable conduct assuming you commendation and prize it for it.

Teaching your dog to "stay" means teaching him or her to remain still until released, even when there are distractions. Getting your dog to sit or lie down, rewarding it with treats, and gradually increasing the duration and distance of the stay are all ways to teach this.

"Down" is the name for teaching your dog to lie down on command. By gradually removing the lure and adding the verbal command "down" while luring your dog into a down position with a treat or toy, this can be accomplished. Your canine will learn that resting when you say "down" is a positive behavior if you praise and reward it for its behavior.

"Come" means teaching your dog to come to you when called, even when they are distracted or off leash. This can be taught by practicing in a calm environment with few interruptions and gradually increasing the distance and interruptions. If you praise and reward your dog for coming when you say "come," it will learn that doing so is a good thing.

"Heel" is a method for teaching your dog to walk by your side calmly and obediently on a loose leash. This can be taught by using positive reinforcement techniques to encourage your dog to walk alongside you and reward good behavior with praise and treats.

It is essential to practice these commands consistently and frequently in a variety of settings to ensure that your dog understands and responds consistently. Utilizing positive reinforcement techniques and avoiding the use of force or punishment, both of which can be detrimental to your dog's bond and counterproductive, are also essential.

In general, one important part of training your dog is teaching him or her basic commands. They can facilitate clear communication between you and your dog, guarantee their safety and good behavior, and prepare them for more advanced training.

In addition to the fundamental commands of obedience, you can teach your German Shepherd additional commands that they will use on a daily basis. One of the most important commands is "Stay." This command is absolutely necessary if you want your dog to remain still while you do things like clean or answer the door. Another significant order that can prevent your canine from eating hurtful things or pursuing creatures is "Leave it."

Teaching your German Shepherd to "heel" is also essential because it will keep them close to you on walks and prevent them from pulling on the leash. "Come" is another useful command that can be used to return your dog to you in the event that they wander off or become distracted.

When teaching your German Shepherd new commands, be patient and consistent. Because dogs learn through repetition and positive reinforcement, rewarding good behavior is essential. To congratulate your dog on their accomplishments, reward them with praise, treats, or toys.

Keep training sessions fun and brief, and avoid using negative reinforcement or punishment, which can cause your dog to become anxious or afraid. With patience, consistency, and positive reinforcement, your German Shepherd can learn all basic obedience commands and become a well-behaved companion.

Once your German Shepherd has mastered the fundamental obedience commands, you can begin teaching them more advanced tricks and behaviors. You could, for example, teach your canine to turn over, pretend to be dead, or shake hands. These tricks are not only fun, but they also strengthen the bond between you and your dog.

When teaching your German Shepherd new tricks, it is essential to break the behavior down into manageable steps and to reward your dog for each successful step. Reward your dog first for lying down, then for turning their head, and finally for rolling over completely if you want to teach your dog to roll over. Molding is a method of training that allows your dog to learn at their own pace without becoming overwhelmed.

Another advanced behavior that your German Shepherd can learn is scent work. Due to their excellent sense of smell, German Shepherds are frequently utilized as police and search and rescue dogs. You can instruct your dog to use their sense of smell to locate hidden objects or even to recognize specific scents, such as those of drugs or explosives.

Setting up your German Shepherd can be a horseplay and remunerating experience for both you and your canine. By starting with basic obedience commands and gradually moving on to more advanced behaviors, you can help your dog become a well-behaved companion and a valuable member of your family.

Socialization

Socialization is a crucial part of raising a well-rounded and well-behaved German Shepherd. Positive and controlled exposure of your dog to a wide range of people, animals, and conditions is part of socialization. By socializing your dog, you can help them gain confidence, lessen their fear and anxiety, and avoid future behavioral issues.

German Shepherds ordinarily start their time of socialization around the age of three weeks and proceed with it until they are roughly four months old. Your puppy should be exposed to as many new things as possible and have positive interactions during this time.

A good way to socialize your German Shepherd with people of all ages, sexual orientations, and races is to introduce them to new people. Offer treats and acclaim for good way of behaving to your loved ones who visit your home and interface with your little dog. It is essential to expose your puppy to children as well because he or she will likely interact with children in the future. When your puppy interacts with children, be kind and patient with him or her, and keep an eye on everything.

Another important aspect of your German Shepherd's socialization is being around other animals. Always do so safely when introducing your puppy to other dogs, cats, and even small animals like rabbits or guinea pigs. When your puppy behaves appropriately and calmly in all interactions with other animals, reward it.

Additionally, your German Shepherd ought to be exposed to parks, bustling streets, and pet stores. As a result of this exposure, your puppy will become more accustomed to new sights, sounds, and smells. However, it is essential to ensure that all vaccinations are current prior to exposing your puppy to other dogs or public areas.

Socialization continues even after your German Shepherd reaches the age of 16 weeks. You must keep introducing your dog to new things throughout their life. Regularly taking your dog for walks, exploring new areas, and introducing them to new animals and people can help with positive socialization and the prevention of behavioral issues.

In conclusion, socialization is an essential part of raising a German Shepherd who is self-assured and well-behaved. By allowing your puppy to interact with a variety of people, animals, and environments in a positive and controlled manner, you can help them become a happy and well-adjusted companion.

The development of your German Shepherd is heavily dependent on socialization. Your canine will learn solid and positive ways of collaborating with different canines and individuals through this interaction. You can assist with forestalling future conduct issues by mingling your pup from the beginning.

In order to socialize your puppy, you must expose it to a wide range of people, animals, and environments. Begin by introducing your dog to your neighbors and friends. Allow them to interact with children, adults, and the elderly. Throughout these interactions, make certain that your puppy is content and at ease.

After that, introduce your puppy to other dogs. Start with dogs that are calm and well-behaved. Gradually introduce your puppy to dogs of varying temperaments, sizes, and breeds. At all times, control and supervise these interactions.

Finally, let your puppy experience a variety of environments. Take them for walks in the park, on the beach, or around the city. Allow them to explore new locations and adapt to new sights, sounds, and smells.

Keep in mind that socialization is a process that never ends and requires patience and persistence. Your doggy ought to be presented to new things all through their life. By doing this, you can help your German Shepherd grow into a well-balanced, self-assured, and content companion.

Socialization includes exposing your puppy to a variety of stimuli. Examples include sounds, surfaces, and even objects. Exposure to new stimuli by a puppy can help prevent anxiety and fear in the future.

Start by introducing your pup to different sounds like traffic, thunder, and fireworks. Puppies can also be introduced to a variety of sounds through sound recordings.

Introduce your puppy to bicycles, hats, and umbrellas among other things. Before allowing your puppy to explore and sniff these items, make sure they are safe and won't harm them.

Introduce your puppy to the different surfaces of grass, sand, and pavement. To get used to the various textures, let them walk on these surfaces.

Watch how your puppy responds to new stimuli to ensure their happiness and comfort. Take a step back and gradually introduce the stimulus to your puppy if they show signs of fear or anxiety.

Keep in mind that socialization includes introducing your puppy to new experiences and teaching them how to behave in social settings. Aggressive or fearful behavior should be discouraged, and positive interactions with humans and other dogs should be encouraged.

By introducing your German Shepherd puppy to other people, you can help prevent future social issues and ensure that they become a trustworthy, respectful, and happy friend.

Crate training

Crate training is a popular and effective method that many dog owners, including German Shepherd owners, use to train their dogs. A container can provide your dog with a safe, comfortable space, help you prepare the house, and prevent your dog from behaving badly.

When crate training your German Shepherd puppy, it's critical to choose the right size crate. Your doggy ought to have the option to stand up, pivot, and rests serenely in the container, yet not so large that they can utilize one region for going to the washroom and the other for dozing.

Leave the door open and place treats and toys inside the case to slowly get your dog used to it. Encourage your puppy to enter the crate by rewarding them for doing so on their own.

Once your puppy gets used to the crate, you can start closing the door for short periods when you are at home. Gradually increase your puppy's time spent in the crate, but make sure they get plenty of opportunities to exercise and go outside for bathroom breaks.

Your little dog ought to have a positive involvement with the container. Your puppy shouldn't be punished with the crate, and you shouldn't leave him or her in it for a long time. Give your puppy plenty of attention, exercise, and socialization outside of the crate.

Crate training can complement house training as well. An appropriately measured carton can urge your little dog to hold their bladder and defecations until they are taken outside since canines normally stay away from ruined dozing regions.

Keep in mind that crate training is a personal choice and not suitable for all dogs. Talk to a seasoned dog trainer or your veterinarian if you have any questions or concerns about carton preparation. Using patience and consistency, you can train your German Shepherd puppy effectively through crate training.

Additionally, crate training can improve your German Shepherd's safety. If you ever need to travel with your dog or take them to the vet, having a case-prepared dog can make the experience much simpler and less stressful for both you and your pet. A container-prepared dog will also be significantly more agreeable and secure in their temporary living quarters if you ever need to bind your dog under any circumstance, such as during a move or home renovation.

It's important to remember that crate training should be done slowly and patiently. You ought to never utilize the carton to rebuff your canine or power it into it. Instead, provide your dog with a cozy and inviting space in the crate. Leave the door open, place their favorite toys and a cushy blanket inside, and let them come and go whenever they want. Your canine ought to be compensated and urged to enter the container all alone from the start. Start by only closing the door for a short amount of time when you're at home and work your way up to leaving your dog in the crate for longer amounts of time when you're away.

Keep in mind that every dog is a one-of-a-kind animal that will respond differently to various training techniques. In your training, be patient and consistent, and always praise good behavior. Your German Shepherd will turn into a thoroughly prepared and polite sidekick with time, exertion, and a lot of commendation.

Additionally, selecting the appropriate case size for your German Shepherd is crucial. Your dog should not have any trouble getting up, turning around, or lying down in the crate; however, it shouldn't be too big that they can use one end as a bathroom and the other as a sleeping area. If you have a puppy, you might need to start with a smaller crate and increase the size as they grow.

Consistency is crucial when it comes to crate training. Your dog should always have access to water and the opportunity to relieve itself outdoors, so adhere to a regular routine. Try not to leave your dog in that state for a very long time because it can cause anxiety and other social problems. If you're going to be away for a long time, you might want to hire a dog walker or pet sitter to get your German Shepherd some exercise.

In addition to crate training, it is essential to provide your German Shepherd with ample physical activity and mental stimulation. Every day, these dogs need to go for walks, runs, or playtime in the backyard because they are very active and have a lot of energy. Beside giving mental and actual excitement, preparing your canine in readiness, acquiescence, or other canine games can likewise reinforce your relationship with your canine.

Although crate training is only one part of general German Shepherd training, it can be a useful tool for making your dog feel safe, at ease, and well-behaved. By practicing patience, remaining consistent, and rewarding success, you can help your German Shepherd become a content and well-adjusted family member.

ADVANCED TRAINING

Advanced training is the next level of German Shepherd training. Once your dog has mastered basic commands and a solid training foundation, you can begin working on more advanced skills and behaviors with him or her. High level preparation is an incredible approach to intellectually and genuinely challenge your canine and fortify your relationship with that person.

Advanced training can take many different forms, depending on what you want to accomplish with your dog. Deftness preparing, high level compliance preparing, insurance preparing, and search and salvage preparing are a few normal sorts of cutting edge preparing for German Shepherds. You can tailor any of these kinds of training to meet your goals and the needs of your dog. Each calls for a different set of abilities and approaches.

Modern preparation can be challenging, but it is also extremely rewarding. As you work on new skills and behaviors, you and your dog will make amazing progress together. With patience, perseverance, and a commitment to positive reinforcement training, you can help your German Shepherd become the best dog they can be and advance their training to the next level.

Before beginning advanced training, it is essential to ensure that your German Shepherd has a solid foundation of fundamental obedience skills. This demonstrates that they are open to working with you in various settings and conditions and that they can reliably answer orders, for example, "sit," "remain," "come," and "heel."

You can start to present more perplexing ways of behaving and exercises to your canine once the individual in question has dominated these essential abilities. Advanced training can keep your dog mentally and physically engaged while also fostering confidence and trust in you as a trainer.

Nevertheless, advanced training should always be approached with caution. This is an essential point to keep in mind. You should only attempt certain types of training under the supervision of a professional trainer because they can be risky if done incorrectly, such as attack or protection training.

Any advanced training you decide to do with your German Shepherd should be done at your dog's pace and with a focus on positive reinforcement. With patience, persistence, and a commitment to forming a strong bond with your dog, you can assist them in reaching their full potential and becoming true superstars in the field of dog training.

A pivotal piece of your German Shepherd's improvement is progressed preparing. At the point when your canine has overwhelmed the fundamental orders and approaches to acting, the opportunity has arrived to take things up an indent and challenge your little man's physical and intellectual abilities.

Most of the time, advanced training involves teaching your German Shepherd new, harder commands and more difficult physical exercises. Examples include advanced obedience, agility, and even training for specialized jobs like search-and-rescue or therapy dog training.

You and your German Shepherd can both benefit from agility training, which is a fascinating and entertaining activity. It requires you to guide your dog through a series of obstacles, including jumps, tunnels, and weave poles. This kind of training has the potential to improve your dog's coordination and self-assurance, in addition to strengthening the bond between you and your canine companion.

Advanced obedience training is based on the fundamental commands sit, stay, and come. New commands that you can teach your German Shepherd include heel, stand, and roll over. You can also teach your dog more advanced skills like jumping through hoops and playing dead. This kind of training can help your dog improve their ability to think critically and focus on a single task for longer periods of time.

Significantly further developed preparing is expected for specific errands like inquiry and salvage and treatment canine preparation. You will need to train your German Shepherd to do specific tasks, like finding scents or comforting people in need, in order to complete these responsibilities. Even though training of this kind takes a lot of time and effort, it can give you a great sense of satisfaction and accomplishment.

Taking everything into account, high level preparation is a fundamental part of the advancement of your German Shepherd. It can strengthen your bond with your fuzzy friend while simultaneously challenging your dog intellectually and physically. Whether you choose to focus on agility, advanced obedience, or specialized tasks, advanced training is sure to be a rewarding experience for you and your German Shepherd.

After your German Shepherd has mastered the fundamental commands for obedience, you might want to move on to more advanced training. Undeniable level readiness can consolidate misleads, sports, and thought capacities that your canine can sort out some way to perform.

Interacting with your dog and keeping their minds active through tricks is a fun and engaging activity. German Shepherds are known to play dead, roll over, and jump through a hoop. It is essential to keep in mind that obedience training should always come first, and that basic commands should always come first.

Your canine can profit from an organized and testing climate in sports like spryness and compliance preliminaries. By requiring your dog to complete particular tasks or navigate obstacle courses, these activities can assist them in developing their obedience skills and improving their physical fitness.

Explicit capacities, for instance, search and rescue or treatment work require a raised level of planning and may not be sensible for all canines. In any case, if your German Shepherd has the perfect character and getting ready, they can be a huge asset in these fields.

No matter what you decide, remember to make advanced training fun and rewarding for your dog. Using positive reinforcement techniques and a lot of praise and treats, your dog can enjoy training and be motivated to learn new skills.

Additionally, it is essential to keep in mind that advanced training should always be carried out with the assistance of a qualified instructor. They can provide you with the tools and techniques necessary to demonstrate your German Shepherd's new skills effectively and safely, and they can also help you investigate any issues that may arise during the preparation phase.

In general, advanced training can be a great way to keep your German Shepherd close to you and physically and mentally active. Your canine can obtain many abilities and stunts that will amaze and dazzle you assuming you show it persistence, devotion, and the fitting preparation techniques.

For German Shepherds, advanced training is a way to test their physical and mental abilities in addition to basic obedience training. In addition, it might give them additional skills that can be useful in a variety of situations. Spryness preparing, aroma and following work, insurance preparing, and different kinds of cutting edge preparing are models.

Agility training is a popular choice for advanced training for German Shepherds. As part of this kind of training, your dog will learn to navigate a course with jumps, tunnels, weave poles, and other obstacles. Agility training can help your dog develop strength, endurance, and coordination in addition to being a fun activity that strengthens the bond between you and your dog.

Another form of cutting-edge preparation that can benefit your German Shepherd is following and aroma work. This kind of training teaches your dog how to track and find specific scents. Tracking and scent work can be used for hunting and search-and-rescue, but it can also be a fun way to work out your dog's instincts and brain.

Helping your canine to safeguard you or your property is a disputable type of cutting edge preparing known as insurance preparing. This kind of training should only be attempted by seasoned instructors, and it should never be used to train a powerful dog. When done precisely, security planning can show your canine balance, quiet submission, and sureness.

An additional form of advanced training is competing in obedience competitions. In obedience competitions, your dog's ability to follow complex commands and perform a variety of tasks with precision and control is tested. Preliminary compliance can provide you and your dog with an additional level of success and security.

In general, advanced training can offer your German Shepherd opportunities to exercise, learn new skills, and stimulate their mind. Similar to any preparation, it is essential to begin with basic acceptance preparation and gradually progress to more challenging exercises. In addition, if you want to try advanced training with your dog, you should always prioritize safety and hire an experienced trainer.

Off-leash training

Off-leash instruction is an essential part of advanced training for German Shepherds. If done correctly, off-leash training can help your dog become more obedient, well-behaved, and confident.

In any case, it is crucial for remember that off-chain preparing ought not be endeavored until your canine knows about wearing a restraint and rope and has learned essential orders. This ensures that you have established a solid foundation of trust and communication with your dog prior to attempting more advanced training methods.

Ensure you have a protected, encased region to work in prior to starting off-rope preparing, similar to a canine park or a fenced terrace. Start by teaching your dog, while they are on a long leash, recall commands like "come" and "here." While rehearsing these orders, bit by bit increment the distance among you and your canine, compensating it with treats and acclaim when it complies.

Once your dog consistently responds to recall commands on a long leash, you can begin practicing off-leash recall in the enclosed area. Start with short distances and gradually increase the distance and duration of the recall exercises. You should always reward your dog for coming when called, even if they were distracted or took a little longer.

Remember that not all canines are reasonable contender for off-rope preparing, especially those with a solid prey drive or a background marked by escaping. Always evaluate your dog's behavior and capabilities prior to attempting off-leash training.

Training your German Shepherd off-leash can be a fun and rewarding way to improve their obedience and strengthen your relationship with them. Your canine can turn into a polite and confident buddy off rope with persistence, consistency, and the right preparation techniques.

A crucial component of cutting-edge training for your German Shepherd is off-chain preparation. After your dog knows basic commands and how to behave around a leash, this kind of training is usually done. Off-leash training teaches your dog to listen to and obey commands without a leash.

The first step in off-leash training is to find a safe place to train your dog. This could be an enormous open space away from occupied streets and interruptions or a closed in yard. A good recall command is essential before beginning off-leash training because your dog should be able to respond immediately when called.

To get started, practice off-leash commands in a setting with little distraction. To reward your dog for accurately responding to your commands, use positive feedback strategies like treats or applause. Start with brief meetings and gradually increase the amount of time spent preparing.

When practicing off-leash training, it is essential to always keep an eye on your dog and your surroundings. Consider using a long chain or a preparation restraint to help you build up your orders if your dog is easily startled or tends to wander.

Consistency is everything when it comes to off-leash training. Be patient with your dog because it will take time to build trust and a strong bond with him or her. Your German Shepherd will figure out how to submit to orders in any event, when off-rope with predictable preparation and uplifting feedback.

Off-leash training can be a fun and rewarding activity for both you and your German Shepherd. Prior to starting off-rope preparing, it is fundamental to guarantee that your canine is completely prepared and respectful while on a chain. When your dog is ready, you must choose a secure location for off-leash training. This could be a dog park, a fence-lined yard, or another secure location.

Consistency and constructive feedback are the keys to successful off-chain preparation. Start with short training sessions and work your way up to longer sessions and more distance. Reward your canine for good way of behaving with uplifting feedback techniques like treats and verbal acclaim. Always conclude the training session with positivity, patience, and perseverance.

When training your German Shepherd off leash, it is essential to keep a close eye on them and be aware of their surroundings. Additionally, you ought to be prepared to intervene when called upon. For example, in case your canine starts to run towards a dangerous district, for instance, a clamoring road, you should rapidly hit them up and put them on a rope.

It is essential to keep in mind that not all dogs are suitable for off-leash training. Some dogs may have a strong desire for prey or be easily distracted, making off-leash training risky or challenging. If you're not sure if your dog is ready for off-leash training, talk to a professional dog trainer.

Overall, off-leash training can be a great way to strengthen your relationship with your German Shepherd and increase their obedience and behavior. You can help your canine in turning into a thoroughly prepared and reliable buddy, both on and off the chain, by rehearsing tolerance, staying predictable, and utilizing uplifting feedback.

Advanced obedience commands

Advanced obedience commands are an essential component of the training process for any German Shepherd dog owner who wishes to have a pet that is well-behaved and obedient. These commands, which go beyond the fundamental ones "sit," "stay," and "come," are frequently used in more difficult situations, such as competitions, or when your dog is off-leash.

Your dog will learn to walk calmly alongside you on a loose leash using the advanced obedience command "heel." One of the most crucial advanced commands is it. This command is especially important for German Shepherds, who can be strong and have a tendency to pull. With the right training, your dog will learn to walk alongside you without pulling or dragging you.

Another important command is the "down-stay" command, which tells your dog to lie down and stay in one place until it is released. You can use this command when you want to eat at a restaurant and need your dog to stay put for a long time, like when you're out in public. With regular training and practice, your dog will learn to remain calm and still until released.

Advanced commands include "Stand," "Come to Heel," "Finish," and "Send Away." Each of these commands has a unique purpose and can be useful in a variety of situations. When you need your dog to move away from you and complete a task at a distance, you can use "send away," while "stand" is used in obedience competitions.

It is essential to keep in mind that advanced obedience training requires basic obedience training as well. Your dog should be able to consistently respond to simple commands like "sit," "stay," and "come" for obedience training. Additionally, motivating your dog with positive reinforcement and rewards is essential to making the training process enjoyable for both of you.

In general, learning advanced commands is necessary for any German Shepherd owner who wants a pet that behaves well and follows instructions. You can show your canine to effectively and unhesitatingly perform progressed orders with persistence, consistency, and encouraging feedback.

Once you have mastered the fundamental commands, you can move on to teaching your German Shepherd advanced obedience commands. To follow these more complex commands, your dog will require more concentration and discipline. However, they can also be extremely rewarding because they enable you to communicate with your dog more effectively and achieve a higher level of obedience.

Some of the most frequently used advanced obedience commands for German Shepherds are as follows:

1. Heel:
Your dog should walk directly alongside you with their shoulder aligned with your leg by obeying the "heel" command. This is an

essential command to have when walking your dog in a crowded area or when you need to watch their movements closely.

2. Stay:

An order called "Remain" tells your dog to stay in one place until you deliver. When you need to leave your dog outside of a store or want to keep him in one place while you do something else, this command is helpful.

3. Come:

Your dog will immediately approach you when you give it the command "Come." This command is absolutely necessary when recalling your dog from dangerous or potentially hazardous situations.

4. Place:

A spot order guides your canine to a foreordained area, like a bed or mat. This command is useful for controlling your dog's movements and keeping them still while you do something.

5. Leave it:

Your dog is instructed to cease interacting with an animal or object by issuing the command "Leave it." This request is significant for holding your canine back from attracting with conceivably hazardous things, as harmful plants or powerful animals.

While showing your German Shepherd advanced accommodation orders, it is crucial for separate the planning into additional unobtrusive advances and logically increase the difficulty. You can urge your canine to get familiar with the new order by utilizing encouraging feedback techniques like acclaim and treats. Be patient and consistent with your preparation as well, as cutting-edge submission orders can take a few weeks or months to fulfill.

By and large, showing your German Shepherd progressed submission orders can assist you with discussing better with your canine and give you more command over their way of behaving and compliance. You can assist your canine with turning into a thoroughly prepared and dutiful friend by showing restraint, staying predictable, and utilizing encouraging feedback.

In addition to the standard commands, you can teach your German Shepherd advanced obedience commands as part of their advanced training. Because they are more intricate, mastering these commands takes more time and patience. Regardless, they are outstandingly important in everyday presence conditions and can help with chipping away at the association among you and your canine.

The "remain" order is one high level of duty that you can demonstrate to your German Shepherd. This command requires your dog to remain in the same position until it is released. To learn the "stay" command, get your dog to sit or lie down first. Then, with your hand out in front of your dog's face, give the command "remain." Give your dog a treat and praise if they remain still as you slowly walk away from them. The time it takes for your dog to stay still and the distance between you and them to increase gradually.

Another general obedience request is the "heel" request. Under this command, your dog must walk close to you on a leash without pulling. To begin teaching your dog the "heel" command, walk him around on a loose leash. As soon as your dog begins to pull ahead, call him or her back to your side. Reward your dog when they return to you and resume walking. Continue onward toward this path until your canine can stroll close by you without pulling.

The "leave it" command is another advanced obedience command that can be very useful in keeping your dog from eating or playing with something that they shouldn't. To begin teaching your dog the "leave it" command, place a treat on the ground and cover it with your hand. By saying "leave it" to your dog, you wait for it to stop being interested. When your dog stops trying to get the treat, reward them with a different treat and praise them. Your dog should be taught to ignore commands by repeating this procedure with a variety of objects.

Advanced obedience commands require patience and consistent practice. After your canine has dominated the basic orders, you ought to just continue on toward the further developed ones. Use only positive reinforcement when training your dog, never aggression or physical punishment. With time and patience, your German Shepherd can become a companion who is obedient and well-behaved.

Agility training

Spryness training is a great way to keep your German Shepherd active and confined. It's a fun and challenging activity that can improve your dog's physical, mental, and coordination skills. Additionally, agility training can help you strengthen your relationship with your dog, improve their sense of self-worth, and provide them with a constructive outlet for their energy.

During agility training, your dog must overcome a variety of challenges and obstacles. These obstacles include jumps, tunnels, weave poles, A-frames, and seesaws. Because the course is timed, your dog should finish it as quickly and accurately as possible. Agility training can be a fun and rewarding activity for you and your German Shepherd, even if it requires a lot of practice and training.

Before beginning agility training with your German Shepherd, it is essential to conduct a health and fitness check. Additionally, you should consult an experienced agility instructor or dog trainer to ensure that you are adhering to the appropriate safety guidelines.

The first step in learning agility is to introduce your dog to each obstacle one at a time. Starting with the least complex hindrance, continuously increment the trouble as your canine additions certainty and solace. Using positive reinforcement techniques like praise and treats, you can encourage your dog and reward them for their progress.

Once your dog is familiar with each obstacle, you can begin combining them into a complete course. Success in agility training requires consistency, patience, and practice. When you work with your dog on a regular basis, you should start with short practice sessions that gradually get longer and more difficult.

In addition to physical training, agility training also includes mental training. Your dog will need to learn how to move through the course by following your instructions. To show your canine these abilities, you can utilize clicker preparing and encouraging feedback.

In general, spryness training is a silly and profitable activity that can help your German Shepherd stay active, engaged, and intellectually sharp. The prizes are certainly worth the work, in spite of the way that it requires tolerance, practice, and consistency. If you want to get started with agility training for your German Shepherd, you might want to consult a professional trainer or sign up for a local agility class.

Agility training is a fun and exciting way to test your German Shepherd's mental and physical abilities. It involves teaching your dog to navigate an obstacle course that includes jumps, tunnels, weave poles, and other challenges. Agility training can help your dog become fitter, more coordinated, and more self-assured as well as a fun way to bond with him.

Before beginning agility training, it is essential to ensure that your dog is in good health and physical condition. Although German Shepherds are well-known for their athletic abilities, you should consult your veterinarian before beginning any new exercise program. Your veterinarian can advise you on your dog's ongoing health and help you determine whether your dog is ready for readiness training.

Once your veterinarian gives you the go-ahead, you can begin gradually introducing your dog to the various agility obstacles. Start with simple obstacles like jumps and tunnels and gradually progress to more challenging ones. Use positive reinforcement techniques like praise and treats when you want to motivate your dog and boost their confidence.

Agility training necessitates patience and consistency because it can take time for your dog to master each obstacle and for you and your dog to work together as a team. You may need to adjust your training methods as your dog progresses through the various levels of agility training. There are a variety of dexterity competitions and classes available, which can provide valuable opportunities for you and your dog to practice and demonstrate your skills.

Remember that agility training should be fun for both you and your dog at all times. Try not to push your dog too much or you might end up disappointed if they don't behave as expected. Always conclude training sessions with a positive note and a brief, enjoyable session. With patience, dedication, and a lot of practice, your German Shepherd can become an expert in agility training while having a great time doing it.

Training your dog in agility is a great way to keep him or her physically and mentally active and to build a stronger bond with them. During agility training, your dog will learn to navigate a course of jumps, tunnels, weave poles, and other obstacles. Even though agility training can be very rewarding, it requires a lot of time, effort, and patience on the part of both you and your dog. This is something that should never be forgotten.

Before beginning agility training, it is essential to ensure that your dog is in good health and has received approval from a veterinarian. To ensure that your dog is training on dependable and secure equipment, you should also invest in high-quality equipment like weave poles, tunnels, and jumps.

In addition to its physical benefits, agility training can enhance your dog's focus and obedience. Through agility training, your dog will learn to follow your commands, stay focused on the task at hand, and better understand the bond between you and your dog.

It's important to start agility training with easy obstacles and work your way up to harder ones over time. To avoid exhausting your dog, you should also break up your training sessions into shorter, more focused ones. Positive reinforcement techniques for keeping your dog motivated and encouraging good behavior include playtime, praise, and treats.

It's critical to remember that not all canines are reasonable for spryness preparing, despite the fact that it tends to be a tomfoolery and compensating action for both you and your canine. Certain breeds, like Border Collies and Australian Shepherds, are frequently better suited for agility training because of their inherent athleticism and high energy. Be that as it may, spryness preparing can be appreciated and valuable by practically any canine with the right preparation and approach.

In general, training your dog in agility can be a great way to keep him or her active and engaged and to improve your relationship with him or her. With patience, practice, and a positive attitude, agility training can provide you and your dog with numerous advantages.

Protection training

A highly specialized form of instruction, dog protection training teaches dogs how to protect their owners and property. German Shepherds are one of the most widely used breeds for protection training due to their intelligence, loyalty, and protective instincts.

Protection training is the process of teaching a dog to respond to commands that will either attack or deter an intruder. The dog learns to recognize danger and act accordingly. This kind of training isn't good for all dogs because it requires a lot of control and discipline.

Protection training begins with obedience training. The dog must have completed basic obedience training before moving on to more advanced protection training. The trainer will instruct the dog to follow commands like sit, stay, come, and heel. This is absolutely necessary to establish trust and control between the trainer and the dog.

The mentor will start acquainting assurance preparing with the canine once the canine is capable in essential compliance. The dog will learn to recognize potential dangers and respond in a controlled and restrained manner to them. The dog must be instructed to attack, hold its ground, and bark on command as part of this.

In order to simulate a real-world scenario, the training will make use of protective equipment like bite sleeves and muzzles. By providing the dog with distractions and other challenges, the trainer will gradually increase the difficulty of the training.

Protection training may not be appropriate for all dogs. The dog's temperament must be suitable for this kind of training, as it requires extreme control and discipline. Additionally, experienced trainers with a thorough understanding of the breed and the necessary training methods should only conduct protection training. This is an important point to keep in mind.

Importantly, a dog should never be taught to be aggressive through protection training. The training shouldn't make the dog aggressive or erratic; rather, it should help the dog recognize and respond to a threat. A thoroughly prepared security canine ought to never represent a danger to its proprietor or others and ought to constantly be confident and devoted.

In conclusion, protection training is a highly specialized discipline and control-intensive form of training. It teaches dogs to behave in a controlled and disciplined manner in order to safeguard their owners' possessions. Because of their knowledge, reliability, and normal defensive impulses, German Shepherds are a well known breed for insurance preparing. Protection training, on the other hand, isn't right for all dogs and should only be done by trained professionals who know a lot about the breed and how to train it.

Training your German shepherd to protect yourself and your belongings is part of protection training, an advanced form of dog training. Keep in mind that only professionals or trained professionals should conduct protection training. This is because the training can be risky and needs to be done carefully to prevent anyone, including the dog, from getting hurt.

During protection training, the dog is taught to be aware of their surroundings, recognize potential dangers, and respond appropriately. Nibble work, in which the canine is educated to chomp and clutch an article or individual until directed to deliver, is one type of this preparation. Another option is to teach the dog to bark and intimidate a potential danger without biting.

Showing the canine fundamental compliance orders and mingling the canine are the most important phases in assurance preparing. The dog needs to be well-socialized and obey commands in order to avoid accidentally attacking someone. The canine has to know the distinction between a real danger and an occurrence in which giving protection isn't required.

After the dog has been socialized and taught basic obedience, it can begin bite work training. The canine is told to snack and grasp a thing or individual until coordinated to convey. The dog is also taught to recognize danger and respond accordingly. The trainer teaches the dog these skills in a variety of ways, such as by using a decoy or a bite sleeve.

Keep in mind that not all German Shepherds are suitable for protection training. Only dogs with stable temperaments and the ability to differentiate between real threats and non-threatening situations should be trained for protection work. Work with a professional trainer to determine whether your dog is suitable for this kind of training.

In conclusion, teaching your German Shepherd how to protect you and your property is the advanced form of dog training known as protection training. This kind of training must be approached with caution and only under the supervision of a trained instructor. If properly trained and socialized, a German Shepherd can be an excellent guard dog; however, not all dogs are suitable for this role.

It is essential for protection training to collaborate with a skilled trainer who can assist you in training your dog safely and effectively. This kind of training should not be attempted by new dog owners because it can be dangerous if done incorrectly.

During protection training, dogs are taught to protect their handler or property at will. This includes obedience training, bite work, and desensitizing the dog to potentially dangerous situations.

An essential component of protection training is the development of the dog's self-assurance. Dogs who require certainty may be reluctant to protect their master or property when called upon. The dog will be worked on by a skilled trainer to improve their confidence and teach them how to speak up when necessary.

Another important aspect of protection training is teaching the dog to bite and then release on command. To keep the canine from turning out to be unnecessarily forceful or perilous, this requires cautious preparation and taking care of. The trainer must also properly train the dog to recognize threats and respond appropriately.

It's important to remember that not all dogs are good candidates for protection training. It's possible that some dogs aren't physically suited to this kind of training, and it's also possible that others don't have the right disposition or drive for it. A reputable trainer will assess the dog's temperament and abilities prior to beginning any protection training.

Protection training can generally be beneficial to those who require additional security and protection. However, it is essential to approach the training with caution and work with an experienced trainer to ensure that it is carried out safely and effectively.

HEALTH AND NUTRITION

Maintaining your dog's well-being and happiness is an essential part of responsible pet ownership. It is essential for your dog's mental and physical health to ensure that they receive adequate nutrition and medical care. Stoutness, diabetes, dental issues, skin issues, and other normal medical problems can be in every way kept away from with great nourishment and clinical consideration.

With the right diet, regular exercise, and medical attention, your dog can live a long and healthy life. It is your responsibility as a dog owner to give your pet the best care possible. Recognizing your dog's nutritional requirements, spotting potential health issues, and seeking appropriate treatment are all necessary for promoting your dog's overall health and wellness.

In this aide, we'll discuss that it is so essential to take care of canines well and deal with them. We will discuss common health issues, the best diet for your dog, the effects of exercise on your dog's health, and how to take your dog to the vet. Whether you are a first-time dog owner or an experienced pet parent, this guide will provide you with useful advice on how to keep your dog healthy and happy.

1. The well-being and happiness of their animal companion is a top priority for any responsible pet owner. One of the most important things you can do is provide them with a well-balanced diet that meets their nutritional needs. This guide covers everything you need to know about feeding a healthy diet to your dog.

2. It is your duty as a pet owner to ensure that your dog gets the nutrients it needs to thrive. Your dog's overall health and well-being depend on its diet. This guide will cover the fundamentals of dog nutrition, such as what to feed your dog, how much to feed them, and how to choose the right food for their specific needs.

3. One of the best ways to keep your dog healthy is to feed them the right food because you are responsible for their health. Nonetheless, with so many canine food decisions out there, it might be hard to advise where to start. This guide will go into detail about dog nutrition to help you choose the right food for your dog.

4. As a dog owner, you want your dog to be content, healthy, and energetic. One of the most important steps you can take to achieve this is to provide them with a diet that is both nutritious and well-balanced. However, what exactly does that imply? We'll go over the intricate details of canine sustenance in this aide, giving you the data you want to go with the most ideal choices for your canine.

Health and proper nutrition are absolutely necessary for raising a healthy puppy. Proper nutrition is essential to ensuring that your dog grows and develops appropriately while maintaining a healthy weight and robust structure. In addition, establishing healthy routines like exercising on a regular basis, grooming, and going to the veterinarian on a regular basis can help catch health problems early.

A diet that is both nutritious and well-balanced is essential for your puppy's health and well-being. Puppies need a diet high in carbohydrates, protein, and fat to help them grow and develop. Your puppy should be fed high-quality commercial dog food that meets their nutritional requirements. The best nourishment for your little dog will rely upon their age, breed, and wellbeing status, so converse with your vet about it.

It is essential to monitor your puppy's weight to ensure that they do not become overweight or stout. An assortment of medical problems, including diabetes, coronary illness, and joint torment, can result from weight. To avoid overfeeding your puppy, follow the feeding instructions on the food label, weigh your puppy frequently, and adjust the portion sizes accordingly. Additionally, avoid feeding your puppy table scraps because this can result in weight gain and an unbalanced diet.

Regular exercise is also necessary for your puppy's health and well-being. Puppies require physical activity to strengthen their muscles, maintain a healthy weight, and stimulate their minds. Exercise can take the form of walking, playing fetch, or any other activity that encourages play and movement. However, it is essential to avoid overworking your puppy's joints and bones because they are still developing and susceptible to injury.

Grooming is another important part of keeping your puppy healthy. They can keep their coat clean and healthy and avoid skin irritations and infections by regularly brushing and bathing. Grooming can also help you find any lumps or abnormalities that might need to be treated by a veterinarian.

Last but not least, regular checkups at the vet are absolutely necessary to maintain your puppy's health. Your veterinarian can provide your puppy with routine vaccinations, monitor his or her growth and age, and detect health issues early. Additionally, your veterinarian may be able to offer advice on exercise, diet, and other health-related issues.

In conclusion, raising a healthy puppy requires a healthy diet and exercise. Regular grooming, exercise, and visits to the veterinarian can all help ensure that your puppy grows and develops appropriately and develops healthy habits throughout their lifetime.

It is essential to ensure that your puppy always has access to clean water in addition to providing a diet that is well-balanced. Change their water every day and make sure their water bowl is always full of clean water. Additionally, to prevent the growth of bacteria, it is recommended to wash the bowl frequently.

The dog's actual activity is an additional aspect of their health to take into consideration. Puppies require a lot of exercise to help them shed excess energy and build strong bones and muscles. Your dog may require more exercise than other dogs, depending on their size and variety. For instance, a Great Dane puppy might need more exercise than a Chihuahua or another smaller breed.

Additionally, your puppy's health depends on regular visits to the veterinarian. Puppies need a series of vaccinations and routine exams to keep an eye on their growth and development and protect them from common diseases. You can also talk to your veterinarian if you have any questions about your puppy's health.

The mental well-being of puppies is just as important as their physical well-being. They require a great deal of socialization and mental stimulation to help prevent boredom and anxiety. Giving your puppy a variety of toys and puzzles to play with and taking them on walks to meet new people and experiences can help keep their minds active.

Remember that no two puppies are the same, so what works for one puppy might not work for another. Based on their behavior and needs, modify your puppy's diet, exercise routine, and mental stimulation. By providing them with a stimulating and healthy environment, you can help your puppy grow into a happy, well-rounded adult dog.

Coming up next are extra ideas for guaranteeing the wellbeing and nourishment of your pup:

1. Regular Vet Visits:

One of the principal parts of staying aware of your pup's prosperity is standard vet check-ups. By identifying any potential health issues early, these visits will assist you in addressing them. Moreover, contingent upon your pup's variety, age, and action level, your veterinarian will actually want to suggest the most appropriate eating regimen.

2. Feeding Schedule:

To oblige their extending bodies, doggies require numerous feasts each day. The majority of puppies will need to eat at least three times per day until they are six months old, though some may need to eat more frequently. Depending on your puppy's appetite and energy levels, make any necessary adjustments and follow the feeding instructions on the food bag.

3. Portion Control:

If you feed your puppy too much, he may become overweight, which could have negative effects on his health. Ensure you give your little dog the perfect proportion of food in view of their age, weight, and action level by utilizing an estimating cup. If you're not sure how much to feed your puppy, talk to your vet.

4. Quality Food:

Your puppy's food's quality and quantity are equally important. Pick a high-quality, nutrient-dense food that is suitable for your puppy's breed and age. Food sources that contain fillers or fake fixings should be avoided because they can be harmful to your dog's health.

5. Fresh Water:

For your puppy's health, he or she must have access to clean, fresh water. Make sure your puppy always has access to clean water and changes it frequently to prevent the growth of bacteria in the bowl.

6. Treats:

Treats can be an extraordinary technique for compensating your pup during getting ready, yet it is fundamental to pick them meticulously. Search for treats that have no fillers or counterfeit fixings and are low in calories. Treats should never account for more than 10% of your puppy's daily calories.

7. Exercise:

Regular exercise is essential for your puppy's mental and physical health. Take your little dog for regular walks or playtime to help them burn off excess energy and maintain a healthy weight.

8. Grooming:

Your puppy's overall health depends on how often you groom it. To keep your puppy's nails from getting too long, trim them and brush their coat often to get rid of dirt and tangles. Brush and floss your puppy's teeth and ears on a regular basis to keep them clean and free of infections.

By following these guidelines, you can assist in ensuring the happiness and health of your puppy throughout their life. Talk to your veterinarian if you have any concerns about your puppy's health or diet.

Feeding your German Shepherd

Feeding your German Shepherd is an essential component of maintaining their well-being and happiness. Because dogs, like humans, require a well-balanced diet to thrive, it is essential to ensure that your pet receives the appropriate nutrients in the appropriate quantities.

Age should be one of your first considerations when giving your German Shepherd food. Puppies require more frequent feedings than adult dogs do, and their diets ought to be tailored to their evolving bodies. Puppies need to be fed three to four times per day until they are six months old. They can then be fed twice daily after that.

A high-quality, nutrient-dense diet that is appropriate for your German Shepherd's age and activity level is essential. Real meat should be the first ingredient in foods with a healthy ratio of protein, fat, and carbohydrates.

Also take into account the particular dietary requirements of your German Shepherd. Dogs with particular medical conditions may, for instance, require diets low in protein or fat. In addition, certain ingredients, such as grains and chicken, should not be included in the diet of some dogs because they may cause sensitivities or allergies.

When determining how much to feed your German Shepherd, it is essential to consider their age, size, and activity level. If you feed your dog too much, it may become obese, which can cause the dog to have joint problems, heart disease, and diabetes. On the other hand, hunger and other medical conditions can result from starvation.

It's just as important to always give your German Shepherd clean, fresh water as it is to choose the right food and portion sizes. Appropriate hydration is necessary for both general health maintenance and avoiding dehydration.

A well-balanced diet is essential for the overall health and wellbeing of your German Shepherd. You can help ensure that your fuzzy friend lives a happy and healthy life by taking into account their specific dietary requirements and giving them the right supplements in the right amounts.

The recurrence of their meals is another important factor to keep in mind when caring for your German Shepherd. Because puppies have smaller stomachs than adult dogs, their stomachs can only hold so much food at once. As a result, puppies will need to be fed more frequently. Puppies should consume three to four small meals per day until they are approximately six months old. After six months, you can gradually introduce two meals per day.

Additionally, it is essential to pay attention to your dog's weight and adjust their portion estimates as necessary. Overfeeding can lead to obesity, which can cause a variety of health issues like diabetes, heart disease, and problems with the joints. On the other hand, underfeeding can lead to malnutrition and a weaker immune system.

Consult your veterinarian if you are unsure of the appropriate level of care for your German Shepherd. Based on your dog's age, weight, and level of activity, they can provide a range.

In addition to the type of food and frequency with which it is fed, it is essential to ensure that your German Shepherd always has access to clean water. Dehydration can have serious effects on your dog's health, so make sure the water bowl is always full of clean water.

In general, feeding your German Shepherd a well-balanced diet and giving them clean water to drink are important for their health and well-being. Talk to your veterinarian if you have any questions or concerns about your dog's diet.

As well as considering the kind of food and dealing with plan for your German Shepherd, it is furthermore basic to zero in on their dietary examples and approaches to acting. Some dogs have a tendency to eat too quickly, which can cause digestive issues like gas and vomiting. Consider feeding your dog smaller, more frequent meals throughout the day or making use of a slow feed bowl to prevent this.

Additionally, it is essential to monitor your dog's weight and adjust their food intake as necessary. Overtraining can lead to weight gain, which puts your dog at risk for a wide range of health issues like diabetes, arthritis, and heart disease. Discuss the appropriate amount of food with your veterinarian to determine your dog's age, weight, and activity level.

Regular exercise and nutritious eating are equally important for your dog's overall health and well-being. German Shepherds need a lot of exercise to stay happy and healthy because they are active dogs. This could be something as simple as a daily run, a walk, or playing in the backyard. Inactivity can lead to boredom, anxiety, and destructive behavior.

A well-balanced and healthy diet, regular exercise, and good medical care can all help your German Shepherd be happy and healthy.

Exercise requirements

Exercise is an essential part of a German Shepherd's life. These dogs require regular mental and physical stimulation due to their high level of activity. Lack of physical activity can lead to boredom, anxiety, and destructive behavior. In this manner, it's vital for sort out the movement requirements of a German Shepherd and allow adequate opportunities to work out.

German Shepherds are energetic dogs who typically require an hour of exercise each day. Strolls, runs, climbs, and yard games are instances of this sort of activity. To keep your dog engaged and interested, it is essential to vary the activities they participate in. Allowing German Shepherds to run free in a safe, fenced area is a great way to give them that opportunity because German Shepherds enjoy running.

Keeping in mind that German Shepherds are more likely than other breeds to have hip dysplasia, a genetic condition that affects the hips, is also essential. Regular exercise can help prevent this condition by strengthening the muscles around the hips. However, it is essential to begin slowly and gradually increase the intensity and duration of exercise to avoid putting too much stress on the joints.

Mental stimulation is just as important as physical activity for German Shepherds. These intelligent dogs thrive in stressful circumstances. Puzzle toys, interactive games, and obedience training are all great ways to keep your German Shepherd's mind active.

In addition, it is essential to monitor your dog's exercise and make any necessary adjustments. If your dog is exhibiting signs of weariness or having trouble walking, it might be a good time to reduce the amount of exercise or time spent doing it. Also, as your dog gets older, their exercise requirements may change, so it's important to change their routine.

A German Shepherd's happiness and health generally depend on how much exercise and mental stimulation they receive. These canines can live lengthy, solid lives and make superb allies for their proprietors assuming that they get sufficient activity.

Regular exercise is crucial to the mental and physical well-being of a German Shepherd. If they don't get enough exercise, they might become restless and bored, which could lead to destructive behavior. The amount and type of exercise your German Shepherd needs may be determined by their age, health, and specific requirements.

Adult German Shepherds need to exercise every day for at least 30 to 60 minutes, whereas puppies need to exercise more frequently but for a shorter amount of time. Playing fetch, walking, jogging, hiking, and other activities can get your German Shepherd moving. Keep them on a rope or in a secure, fenced area to prevent them from running away and getting into dangerous situations.

Physical activity and mental stimulation are crucial to a German Shepherd's health. They can stay mentally sharp and avoid boredom by participating in mind-testing activities like games, training sessions, and puzzle toys.

It is essential to keep in mind that your German Shepherd's exercise plan might need to be modified to accommodate certain injuries or health conditions. Always consult your veterinarian before beginning a new exercise program or making significant adjustments to their current routine.

Another way to get your German Shepherd moving is to get them involved in interactive play. Playing games like "get," "back-and-forth," and "find the stowaway" can be a fun way to train your dog and strengthen your bond. Playing intelligently can also help your dog grow intellectually, which is important for their overall health.

Keep in mind that the amount of exercise your dog needs will depend on his age, size, and health. Physical activity needs will differ for dogs of all ages, from puppies to senior dogs. Talk to your vet whenever you want to find out how much exercise your German Shepherd needs.

Exercise and good nutrition are just as important for your dog's overall health. A diet that is nutritious and well-balanced can help your German Shepherd stay healthy and in good physical condition.

When selecting dog food, look for a high-quality brand designed specifically for large breed dogs. It is essential to provide German Shepherds with food rich in glucosamine and chondroitin in order to maintain the health of their joints because of the dog's susceptibility to certain health issues like hip dysplasia.

In addition, it is essential to feed your dog the appropriate amount of food for their age, weight, and activity level. Over-burdening can incite weight and other ailments, while starving can provoke hunger.

In addition to their regular meals, you can provide your German Shepherd with healthy snacks like fruits and vegetables. Green beans, apples, and carrots are all good options. You should not feed your dog chocolate, onions, grapes, or any other food that can be harmful to dogs.

Last but not least, it is absolutely necessary to guarantee that your German Shepherd will always have access to clean, new water. Because dehydration can result in serious health issues, ensure that your dog has access to water at all times, particularly during and after exercise.

Grooming

A German Shepherd needs to be groomed on a regular basis. Due to its thick double coat, this breed sheds a lot, especially during the shedding season. Grooming your dog on a regular basis will not only help keep him or her clean and healthy, but it will also cut down on the amount of fur that gets on your clothes and furniture.

Brushing your German Shepherd's coat is the first step in grooming it. The coat can be kept shiny and healthy by brushing it once or twice a week, preventing mats and tangles. A slicker brush or undercoat rake is ideal for removing loose fur and preventing matting. Starting at the head, work your way down the body brushing in the direction of hair growth. Make sure to pay special attention to places where mats and tangles are likely to form, like under the legs and behind the ears.

To avoid stripping the normal oils from your German Shepherd's coat, washing him or her should only be done when absolutely necessary. If your dog has rolled in something unpleasant, you may need to bathe them more frequently than once every three months. After bathing, use a gentle dog shampoo and thoroughly rinse to avoid irritating their skin.

To prevent your German Shepherd's nails from becoming excessively long, which can result in pain or even injury, regular nail trimming must be performed in addition to brushing and bathing. You can trim your dog's nails with a guillotine-shaped nail clipper or a Dremel tool. To prevent pain and bleeding, make the cut as close to the quick as you can.

In addition, German Shepherds must regularly have their teeth cleaned to prevent tooth decay and gum disease. You can give them dental chews and toys that help keep their teeth healthy, or you can brush their teeth with a toothbrush with soft bristles and toothpaste that is safe for dogs.

Last but not least, clean your German Shepherd's ears on a regular basis. The accumulation of wax and debris can result in infection and discomfort. Using cotton balls or pads and a gentle ear cleaner, clean the inside of the ear. Be careful not to put anything heavy in the ear canal because doing so could hurt.

In conclusion, grooming is an essential part of taking care of a German Shepherd. By practicing regular grooming, you can improve your dog's health, comfort, and appearance.

Grooming your German Shepherd on a regular basis is crucial to its health and well-being. Your dog's grooming routine will vary depending on the length and texture of its coat, but all German Shepherds require the same fundamental care.

The most important thing to do is brush your German Shepherd's coat on a regular basis. This forestalls mat development and assists with eliminating soil and free fur. Manage the coat beginning at the head and working your direction down to the tail with a slicker brush or brush. Pay close attention to the animal's legs, belly, and behind the ears, which are the longer areas of its fur. Regular brushing also helps spread out the natural oils in your dog's coat, which keeps it healthy and shiny.

In addition to brushing, your German Shepherd will need regular baths to keep its coat clean and healthy. Make use of a high-quality dog shampoo and conditioner designed specifically for their coat type. Rinse the coat thoroughly to remove all shampoo, as any residue can irritate the skin.

Grooming also includes trimming your nails. Long nails can be uncomfortable and painful, and they may also damage your furniture and floors. Your German Shepherd's nails should be trimmed twice a month, depending on how quickly they grow. With a sharp, high-quality nail clipper, be careful not to cut too close to the quick, the blood vessel of the nail.

Last but not least, ensure that the ears and teeth of your German Shepherd are regularly cleaned. Be careful not to get anything into the ear canal when wiping the ears with a soft cloth or cotton ball. Use a dog-specific toothbrush and toothpaste to prevent dental issues.

Grooming is an important part of your German Shepherd's overall health and wellness care. You can help your canine look and feel their best by adhering to a standard prepping plan.

Maintaining regular checkups of your German Shepherd's teeth, eyes, and ears is just as important as brushing and grooming them.

Inspect their ears for any swollenness, release, or redness. After gently cleaning their ears with a damp cloth or cotton ball, be sure to thoroughly dry them to prevent moisture buildup, which could result in an infection.

Check their eyes for any redness, swelling, or discharge. If you notice anything unusual, you should talk to your veterinarian for advice. Make an effort to manage the fur around their eyes to prevent it from irritating or piercing them.

In the end, take care of your German Shepherd's gums and teeth. Regular use of a dog-specific toothbrush and toothpaste can help prevent tooth decay and tartar buildup. Dental bites or bones can aid the cleaning of their teeth and energize solid biting propensities.

A crucial component of overall care for your German Shepherd is grooming. Grooming them on a regular basis will help you keep them healthy, happy, and looking their best.

Common health issues and how to prevent them

German Shepherds are generally healthy, despite the fact that all breeds are susceptible to certain health issues. If you are aware of these issues and how to avoid them, you can keep your German Shepherd happy and healthy for many years to come.

One of the most common health problems affecting German Shepherds is hip dysplasia. This genetic condition affects the hip joints, causing them to become unstable and loose. This can make it difficult for the dog to walk or even stand up in severe cases, resulting in arthritis and pain. If you want to avoid hip dysplasia in your German Shepherd, you must purchase it from a reputable breeder that checks their breeding dogs for it.

Another common health problem in German Shepherds is bloat. The stomach twists and overflows with gas in this condition, which can lead to a blockage that could kill you. Bloat is most common in German Shepherds, large dogs with deep chests, and it can be caused by eating too quickly, drinking too much water, or exercising immediately after eating. To prevent bloating in your German Shepherd, you should feed them smaller meals throughout the day, do not give them water right before or after meals, and wait at least an hour before exercising after meals.

Moreover, German Shepherds are defenseless to sensitivities, which can appear as tingling, redness, and skin bothering. Allergies can be brought on by food, pollen, dust, and other elements in the environment. To prevent allergies, your German Shepherd should be fed a high-quality diet free of common allergens like wheat, soy, and corn. Their environment should also be kept as clean as possible and free of allergens.

Ear contaminations, dental issues, and skin diseases are extra medical problems that can influence German Shepherds. Getting regular veterinary checkups, maintaining good hygiene, eating a nutritious diet, and getting plenty of exercise can all help protect your German Shepherd's health from these and other problems.

It is essential to recognize your German Shepherd's illness symptoms in addition to taking preventative measures so that you can take them to a veterinarian as soon as possible. Common signs of illness in dogs include lethargy, vomiting, diarrhea, loss of appetite, coughing, and difficulty breathing. You should see a vet right away if your German Shepherd shows any of these symptoms.

Another common health issue in German Shepherds is hip dysplasia. Here, the hip joint doesn't grow as it should, so the bones rub against each other, causing pain and agony in the joint. Hereditary qualities or natural elements like heftiness or quick development can prompt hip dysplasia. For the purpose of preventing hip dysplasia, it is essential to select a reputable breeder that screens their dogs. Hip dysplasia hazard can likewise be diminished by keeping a solid weight and not workaholic behavior during the development stage.

Another common health issue in German Shepherds is bloat, a life-threatening condition in which the stomach twists on itself and traps air and food. This could cut off blood supply to the stomach, resulting in tissue damage and shock. Bloating can be caused by eating too much, eating too quickly, or exercising immediately after eating. To hinder swell, it's crucial for deal with your German Shepherd more humble meals throughout the day, avoid work on following galas, and beat quick eating by using puzzle feeders or dealing with additional unassuming partitions even more routinely down.

Sensitivities and diseases of the skin are likewise normal in German Shepherds. Allergies can be brought on by food, pollen or dust from the environment, flea bites, or both. Allergies may cause itchiness, redness, and hair loss. Infection symptoms include itchiness, redness, discharge, and odor. To avoid skin problems, it's important to keep your German Shepherd clean and groomed, protect them from fleas and ticks, and eat a healthy diet.

Finally, certain eye conditions, such as moderate retinal degeneration and waterfalls, are more common in German Shepherds. Genetic, these circumstances much of the time bring about vision misfortune or visual deficiency. Through routine eye examinations, a veterinary ophthalmologist can assist in identifying and monitoring these conditions.

In addition to the usual health issues, German Shepherds may also be susceptible to epilepsy, heart disease, and cancer. Your German Shepherd's long and happy life can be ensured by living a healthy lifestyle, regularly visiting the veterinarian, and keeping an eye out for any changes in behavior or appearance.

Bloat is yet another serious health issue that can affect German Shepherds. This condition can be fatal if the stomach fills with gas and twists, cutting off blood supply to the stomach and other organs. This condition can be prevented by feeding your dog smaller meals throughout the day and avoiding exercise and playtime immediately following meals.

Additional health conditions that frequently affect German Shepherds include allergies, ear infections, dental issues, and skin infections. Regular visits to your veterinarian and good hygiene can help prevent these issues from becoming more serious health issues.

In conclusion, taking care of your German Shepherd's health and well-being is essential if you want it to live a happy and fulfilling life. By providing a healthy diet, regular exercise, proper grooming, and preventative medical care, you can help your beloved pet live a long   and   healthy   life.

TROUBLESHOOTING

With regards to preparing a canine, not all things will go as expected. Even the most well-trained and well-behaved German Shepherds can sometimes act in a problematic way. This is where troubleshooting comes into play.

During your German Shepherd's preparation, investigating is the method involved with recognizing and settling any issues that might emerge. It includes perceiving tricky way of behaving, fathoming why it happens, and finding answers for aid its remedy.

Dog owners must be aware that one common phase of training is troubleshooting. When working through issues, patience and perseverance are also essential because some may take longer to resolve than others.

In this section, we'll tell you how to deal with some of the most common problems German Shepherd owners might run into during training. We'll talk about everything, from pulling on the leash to separation anxiety to barking and biting.

German Shepherd owners need to be aware that even if their dog is well-trained and behaves well, there will be times when they run into problems. Troubleshooting is the process of identifying and resolving issues with your dog's behavior or health.

Many German Shepherd owners struggle with separation anxiety. This can be seen in dogs that become agitated and destructive when left alone. It is essential to gradually acclimate your dog to being left alone for brief periods before gradually increasing this time in order to resolve this issue. You can also provide your dog with numerous toys and activities if you want to keep them occupied while you are away.

Another possibility is destructive behavior. German Shepherds require a lot of exercise and mental stimulation because they are active dogs. If they don't get enough exercise, they could become destructive and bored. It is essential to provide your dog with ample playtime and exercise to avoid this issue.

Furthermore, a few German Shepherds might show forceful way of behaving toward different canines or people. If your dog exhibits aggressive behavior, it is essential to address the issue as soon as possible. This could mean working with a professional behaviorist or coach to help your dog learn how to connect with other people in a good way.

In addition to behavioral issues, German Shepherds may have health issues. One of the most prevalent health issues is hip dysplasia, a genetic condition that affects the hips and can hinder mobility and cause pain. It is essential to select a reputable breeder who checks their dogs for hip dysplasia and to provide your dog with a healthy diet and regular exercise in order to maintain a healthy weight and support joint health.

Another common health issue that affects German Shepherds is allergies. This can manifest itself in a variety of ways, such as digestive issues or skin irritation. The issue can be managed by figuring out what caused the allergy and treating it with something like a new diet or medication.

Another common issue that many dog owners face is destructive behavior. Examples include digging holes in the yard, barking excessively, and chewing on furniture and other household items. Boredom or anxiety frequently motivate this behavior, which can be changed with more exercise, mental stimulation, and training.

Fear of being abandoned is another common problem that can manifest itself in disastrous behavior, extreme yelling or crying, and, surprisingly, actual side effects like vomiting or loose bowel movement. Separation anxiety treatment can be challenging and may require the assistance of a trained dog trainer or behaviorist. However, steps like gradually increasing the amount of time the dog is allowed to be alone, providing a lot of toys and mental stimulation, and creating a pleasant and comfortable environment can help reduce side effects.

Finally, aggressive behavior can be a serious issue that requires immediate attention. Growling, biting, or other aggressive behavior directed at other dogs or people may be signs of this. Hostility should be treated promptly with the assistance of an experienced mentor or behaviorist because it can have a variety of fundamental causes, such as trepidation, uncertainty, or dominance issues. Dependent upon the earnestness of the aggression, the leaders methodologies, changing on a surface level, or remedy may mean a lot to watch both the canine and others.

In some cases, behavioral issues may necessitate the assistance of a dog behaviorist or trainer. Issues like fearing abandonment, exorbitant woofing, horrendous biting, and animosity toward individuals or different canines are instances of ways of behaving that might require particular preparation and changing on a surface level strategies.

It implies a considerable amount to address direct issues when they arise, as they can become instilled after some time and more testing to address. You and your canine can team up with a behaviorist or coach to think up a custom tailored preparing methodology that resolves the specific main issue.

In addition to behavioral issues, other health or medical conditions may influence your dog's behavior. Changes in behavior, for example, can be brought on by certain illnesses like hypothyroidism or constant pain. If you're concerned about your dog's behavior, you should talk to your veterinarian about it to avoid major medical problems.

When attempting to troubleshoot your German Shepherd, a combination of appropriate training, behavior modification, medical intervention, and ongoing monitoring and evaluation may be required. By collaborating closely with your German Shepherd and utilizing the appropriate resources, you can assist him or her in overcoming obstacles and leading a healthy and happy life.

Behavioral issues and how to correct them

Despite our adoration for our German Shepherds, they may still exhibit behavioral issues. German Shepherd owners may encounter a number of common behavioral issues with their dogs, including aggressive behavior, separation anxiety, destructive chewing, excessive barking, and contaminating the house.

Individuals, different canines, or different creatures can be generally the objectives of hostility. This could be due to fear, dominance, or territoriality. Destructive behavior, excessive barking, and even self-injury are additional common signs of separation anxiety. Destructive chewing is frequently triggered by boredom, anxiety, or frustration. Excessive barking can indicate fear, boredom, or territorialism. In the end, house destruction may be the result of inadequate preparation or medical issues.

It is essential to comprehend the underlying cause of the behavioral problem in order to effectively address it. With the right training, exercise, and mental stimulation, the issue can frequently be resolved. If you give your German Shepherd enough activity and mental stimulation, it can help prevent damaging biting, unreasonable yelling, and dirtying the house. Crate training can also help alleviate separation anxiety.

When dealing with aggression, it is essential to collaborate with a professional dog trainer who is able to evaluate your dog's behavior and develop a training plan that addresses the underlying cause. In some cases, medication may be required to alleviate the dog's anxiety.

In every circumstance, consistency and patience are essential. When working on social issues with your German Shepherd, it's important to keep cool and assertive. Your dog's anxiety will only get worse if you punish him or her and yell at him. Preparing with treats and applause known as encouraging feedback can be extremely viable in resolving social issues.

It is essential to keep in mind that every dog is distinctive and may call for a variety of behavioral management techniques. If you are having trouble resolving a behavioral issue with your German Shepherd, you can get individualized guidance and support from a professional dog trainer or behaviorist.

Another common behavioral issue that dogs face is separation anxiety. When a dog with separation anxiety is left alone or separated from its owner, it experiences extreme anxiety. Separation anxiety is characterized by excessive barking, whining, destructive behavior, and even inappropriate urination. It is crucial for remember that these side effects can likewise be welcomed on by different variables, like weariness, inertia, or deficient preparation.

In order to help treat separation anxiety, gradually getting your dog used to being left alone for longer periods of time is essential. This can be achieved by beginning with a short measure of time burned through alone with your canine and progressively expanding it more than half a month. It's important to give your dog a lot of exercise and mental stimulation to keep him from getting bored.

Aggression is yet another serious issue that can arise in a dog's behavior. Conduct that is forceful can be aimed at different canines, individuals, or different creatures. To appropriately address the animosity, it is essential to identify its cause. A history of abuse or inadequate training, on the other hand, can result in aggression toward humans, as can fear or a lack of socialization.

You should immediately seek professional assistance if your dog behaves aggressively. An expert behaviorist or dog trainer can help you figure out the cause of the issue and come up with a plan to fix it. In some cases, medication may be required to help control the aggressive behavior.

A dog's behavior can be affected by a number of medical conditions in addition to these behavioral issues. Discomfort or pain, for instance, can set off a dog's irritability and aggression. Take your dog to a veterinarian for evaluation if you observe any significant or sudden behavioral changes.

One more difficult issue with a canine's way of behaving that can jeopardize the canine and those around it is hostility. If your German Shepherd exhibits aggressive behavior toward other animals or people, it is essential to seek professional assistance from a certified dog trainer or behaviorist. They can help identify the underlying causes of the aggression and develop a training plan to address them.

In addition to these typical behavioral issues, German Shepherds may also struggle with leash pulling, jumping on people, and excessive barking. You can solve these issues with patience, consistency, and positive reinforcement with the right training.

It is essential to keep in mind that every dog is unique and may require a different behavioral treatment plan. Prior to endeavoring to resolve any serious social issues all alone, consistently counsel an expert.

In conclusion, being able to deal with behavioral issues in German Shepherds is essential for responsible dog owners. If you are aware of the most common behavioral issues these dogs face and take an active approach to training and socialization, you can help prevent and correct problematic behaviors. Also, don't be afraid to ask a trained professional for help if you run into more serious problems. With the right care and training, your German Shepherd can live a happy and well-behaved life.

Training for specific situations (e.g. car rides, visitors, etc.)

A significant piece of your German Shepherd's preparation is preparing for explicit circumstances. By exposing your dog to a variety of situations, you can assist him or her in becoming a well-behaved and self-assured dog. He or she will be able to avoid developing problematic behaviors as a result of this. Some exhortation on the best way to set up your German Shepherd for explicit circumstances is as per the following:

1. Car Rides:

Train your German Shepherd to be cool headed in the vehicle in the event that they become restless or awkward in the vehicle. Get your dog acclimated to being in and around the vehicle first, then gradually introduce short rides in the vehicle. Positive feedback should be used to encourage good behavior, and the length of the rides should always be increased.

2. Visitors:

If your German Shepherd barks or acts aggressively toward visitors, teach them to be calm and friendly. Start by inviting a friend or family member over with your dog on a leash. Treats can be used to reward good behavior, and the number of guests should always increase.

3. Children:

Teaching your German Shepherd to be gentle and patient with children is essential. Start by introducing your dog to the kids while you control them and they are calm. Teach your dog to associate positive experiences with all of the children's interactions.

4. Other Dogs:

If your German Shepherd becomes anxious or aggressive when they are around other dogs, it is essential to socialize them and teach them how to behave appropriately around them. Start by introducing your dog to other dogs in a safe environment like a dog park or training class. Use positive reinforcement and gradually lengthen interactions to encourage good behavior.

5. Loud Noises:

If your German Shepherd is afraid of loud noises like fireworks or thunderstorms, it is important to de-sensitize them. Play recordings of these sounds to your dog at a low volume at first, increasing the volume gradually over time. Positively reinforce calm behavior and gradually increase the duration of exposure.

Training your German Shepherd for car rides can be very helpful in another important situation. Numerous dogs have a fear of driving, which can be stressful for the dog and its owner. Notwithstanding, you can assist your German Shepherd with feeling more calm and certain about the vehicle with the right preparation.

One technique for starting readiness your German Shepherd for vehicle rides is to familiarize them with the vehicle in a positive way. Begin by allowing your dog into the vehicle with you while it is parked and turned off. Reward them with treats or praise when they join you in the car. When your dog accepts this, you can gradually increase the amount of time you leave the vehicle on while they are inside by turning it on and off while they are inside.

As a next step, take your dog on short car rides around the block or to a nearby park. To keep your dog occupied and distracted throughout the ride, bring plenty of treats and toys. If your dog becomes restless or afraid during the ride, stop the vehicle and let them calm down before continuing.

Furthermore, appropriately getting your canine in the vehicle while driving is fundamental. This can be done with a crate or a car harness. Not only does this safeguard your dog, but it may also make them feel more secure during the ride.

At the point when guests visit your home, preparing can likewise be helpful. Some dogs can become territorial or fearful when strangers enter their home, which can lead to aggression or other undesirable behaviors.

To get your German Shepherd ready for visitors, start by teaching them basic obedience commands like "sit," "stay," and "come." Once your dog has mastered these commands, practice them with new friends and family members.

During these training sessions, reward your dog for good behavior and use commands like "no" or "leave it" to redirect any bad behavior. Your German Shepherd ought to turn out to be more calm and confident around guests to your home with training.

In addition to these specific circumstances, it is essential to continue training your German Shepherd throughout their lifetime to maintain good behavior and avert undesirable behavior. Your German Shepherd's happiness and well-being may be aided by regular training, consistent discipline, and positive reinforcement.

It means a lot to show your German Shepherd how to act around individuals and different creatures as well as preparing for explicit circumstances. Preparation for socialization should begin very early to help your dog become comfortable with new people, animals, and environments. This will help prevent aggressive behavior and tension in unfamiliar situations.

You can acquaint your canine with new individuals, pets, and conditions through socialization preparing. Introduce your German Shepherd to new sights, sounds, smells, and experiences gradually in a positive and controlled manner. Good behavior can be rewarded with treats and praise, and bad behavior can be redirected with commands and corrections.

It is likewise vital for remember that a guaranteed canine coach or behaviorist might be expected to help with specific social issues. Look for proficient help in the event that your German Shepherd displays forceful way of behaving or diligent social issues.

By and large, you really want persistence, consistency, and devotion to prepare your German Shepherd. With the right training methods and a positive attitude, you can help your dog become a companion who is well-behaved and obedient.

Dealing with aggression

Because dealing with dog aggression can be difficult, having an understanding of the various forms of aggression is essential. Fear, resource guarding, territoriality, or dominance over other dogs in their social group may all cause some dogs to act aggressively. It is essential to identify the underlying cause of the aggression before choosing a course of action.

If your German Shepherd exhibits aggressive behaviors, you must seek professional assistance from a certified dog trainer or behaviorist. They will be able to look at the situation and come up with a unique plan to stop the aggression.

As a general rule, it is essential to avoid responding negatively to your dog's aggressive behavior because doing so frequently exacerbates the situation. All things considered, it's important to show your dog other options and more appropriate behaviors. This could incorporate desensitization and counter-molding practices in which your canine is step by step presented to what causes their hostility in a positive, controlled climate.

Establishing yourself as the pack leader is also essential because dogs are social animals that respond well to clear boundaries and expectations. Dutifulness preparation, which can assist in establishing a relationship of respect and trust between you and your dog, can be used to accomplish this.

If your dog acts aggressively toward other dogs or strangers, you should always keep them under your control and on a leash. Restricting your canine's openness to circumstances that cause hostility may likewise be important.

In severe cases of aggression, your dog may require medication to manage their behavior. Nonetheless, this ought to just be endeavored if all else fails and under the oversight of a certified behaviorist or veterinarian.

Managing aggression in a German shepherd can be challenging and upsetting, but with patience, dedication, and professional assistance, this issue can be managed and even overcome.

In addition to the steps outlined above, it is essential to seek professional assistance from a dog trainer or animal behaviorist if the aggression issue does not improve or persists despite your efforts. A qualified professional can evaluate your dog's behavior and develop a bespoke training plan to address the underlying causes of aggression.

Keep in mind that dealing with aggression can be difficult and time-consuming, but with patience and consistent effort, you can help your dog become a well-behaved and well-adjusted member of your family. Additionally, it is essential to keep your cool and refrain from physically punishing your dog because doing so could exacerbate the situation and damage your relationship with it.

Another effective method for dealing with aggression in a German Shepherd is to follow a predetermined routine. German Shepherds are intelligent dogs who thrive on structure and routine, which can assist them in avoiding aggressive behavior and reducing anxiety.

Part of a structured routine might be to schedule feeding, exercise, and training at specific times. It's also important to have a set of rules and expectations for your German Shepherd's behavior that are consistent. For instance, if your dog is not permitted on the sofa, consistently implement that rule.

While managing German Shepherd hostility, consistency is fundamental. If you allow your dog to act aggressively in some situations but not others, it may confuse it and make the aggression worse. Everyone should always adhere to the house rules and behavior expectations for your German Shepherd.

Additionally, your German Shepherd ought to be socialized appropriately from a young age. As part of its socialization, your dog needs to be exposed to a wide range of people, animals, and environments in a positive and controlled way. This might help with forestalling forceful way of behaving toward outsiders or creatures.

If your German Shepherd is being aggressive toward other animals or people, you need to get professional help from a licensed dog trainer or behaviorist. They can look at what's going on and come up with a new strategy to fix the problem.

In some cases, German Shepherds' aggression may necessitate medication. However, this should only be used under the direction of a veterinarian and in conjunction with training for behavior modification.

Dealing with a German Shepherd's aggression can be difficult and stressful. In any case, it is possible to address and control aggressive behavior with persistence, consistency, and the right approach.

In some cases, professional assistance may be required when dealing with German Shepherd aggression. A specialized dog behaviorist or trainer can examine the dog's behavior and develop a bespoke training strategy to address the issue. Selecting a qualified professional with prior experience working with aggressive dogs is crucial.

While dealing with German Shepherd hostility, there are some general guidelines to keep in mind in addition to expert assistance. The main thing is to stay mentally collected and try not to respond with dread or fury, which can exacerbate things. Instead, lead calmly and confidently by issuing commands that are consistent and clear.

The dog should not be punished for being aggressive because doing so could make the behavior worse. Focus instead on positive reinforcement training, which involves rewarding the dog for good behavior and gradually decreasing their susceptibility to aggressive situations.

Make sure the dog gets enough exercise and mental stimulation because boredom and stored energy can cause aggression. Socialization and normal acquiescence preparing can likewise assist with preventing forceful way of behaving from occurring in any case.

In some cases, medication may be prescribed to help control the dog's aggression. However, only under the supervision of a veterinarian should this be attempted on its own.

It tends to be troublesome and possibly perilous to manage hostility in a German Shepherd, however it is feasible to oversee and address the way of behaving with persistence, consistency, and expert help if essential.

Figuring out the fundamental reasons for canine animosity and attempting to address them through uplifting feedback, reliable preparation, and persistence are eventually the keys to settling the issue. With time and effort, you can help your dog overcome its aggressive behavior and become a happy, healthy, and well-adjusted companion.

Conclusion

Overall, German Shepherd training is a lengthy process that requires investment, perseverance, and commitment. A well-trained German Shepherd can be a useful member of the family, a reliable friend, and a protector. Fundamental dutifulness orders, high level acquiescence orders, deftness preparing, assurance preparing, wellbeing and nourishment, prepping, investigating, and managing conduct issues and hostility are completely canvassed in this conclusive manual for German Shepherd preparing.

You can foster a positive relationship with your German Shepherd and encourage them to be courteous and obedient by adhering to the suggestions and techniques presented in this guide. Preparation should never include harsh or correctional methods and should always be a positive experience for both you and your dog. Consistency, patience, and positive reinforcement can help your German Shepherd achieve their full potential and foster a strong bond with you.

Keep in mind that every German Shepherd is different, so different training methods might be needed for each one. Be flexible in your preparation strategies and concentrate on your dog's unique needs and behaviors. With time and effort, you can help your German

Shepherd become a companion who is content, healthy, and well-behaved.

German Shepherds are highly intelligent and adaptable dogs, so proper training is necessary for them to live a happy and healthy life. As a responsible owner, it is essential to train your dog using positive reinforcement techniques and address any behavioral issues that may arise.

Teaching your dog basic commands, advanced obedience, agility, or protection training requires patience, consistency, and firmness. By exercising your German Shepherd on a regular basis, feeding it a well-balanced diet, and properly grooming it, you can help to ensure that it is healthy, content, and well-behaved.

In addition, it is essential to be well-prepared for particular situations, such as traveling in a car, receiving visitors, and dealing with aggressive behavior. You can guarantee that you have an ally until the end of your life who gives you pleasure and satisfaction by acquiring a comprehension of your canine's way of behaving and attempting to resolve any issues.

The Conclusion of German Shepherd Training: The Ultimate Guide has everything you need to know about how to train and care for your German Shepherd. You can raise a cheerful, solid, polite canine that is a delight to be near assuming that you follow the proposals in this book. Keep in mind that training your German Shepherd is a never-ending process that requires patience, consistency, and a lot of love, but the rewards are definitely worth the effort.

Recap of key training techniques

Because of their intelligence, loyalty, and adaptability, German Shepherds are ideal for a wide range of training. When training your German Shepherd for obedience, protection, agility, or any other purpose, there are a few key techniques you should keep in mind to ensure that your dog learns safely and effectively.

One of the most crucial strategies is the use of positive reinforcement. Positive reinforcement is the practice of rewarding good behavior with treats, praise, or other incentives instead of punishing bad behavior. You can show your German Shepherd that specific activities bring about certain results by utilizing encouraging feedback. Your dog will be more likely to repeat those actions in the future because of this.

Another important technique is consistency. Every time you train your dog, you should use the same commands, rewards, and methods to avoid confusing or frustrating him or her. To keep good habits from developing and to reinforce those that are already present, consistency also implies that you should train your dog on a regular basis.

Socialization is another important part of training a German Shepherd. Socialization involves exposing your dog to a variety of people, animals, and conditions so that it learns how to behave appropriately in different situations. German Shepherds need a lot of socialization because they can be protective of their owners and suspicious of strangers or new animals.

Another important strategy is leash training. Helping your dog walk calmly on a chain without pulling or pulling is rope training. It is essential to train your dog to walk on a leash not only for your convenience but also for the safety and comfort of your dog.

Last but not least, it's important to remember that no two dogs are the same and that some might need more or less training than others. Some dogs may be able to pick up new skills quickly and easily, but others may have particular problems or difficulties that call for specialized training methods.

In a nutshell, successful training of German Shepherds requires positive reinforcement, consistency, socialization, leash training, and individualized training methods. Using these methods and tailoring your training to your dog's specific requirements and abilities, you can help your German Shepherd become a companion who is well-behaved, content, and obedient.

Keep in mind that every German Shepherd is unique and responds differently to different preparation methods as you continue to prepare them. Consequently, it is essential to maintain a fluid and adaptable approach.

In addition to the methods described above, positive reinforcement methods like treats, verbal praise, or playtime should always be used to reinforce good behavior. Consistency, patience, and a positive attitude are essential for successful training.

In addition, it is crucial to continue training your dog throughout its entire life—not just while it is still a puppy. Regular training sessions can help your dog's mental stimulation and behavior.

Last but not least, if you encounter difficulties with your preparation that you are unable to resolve on your own, it is essential to seek professional assistance. A certified dog trainer's expert guidance and support can help you and your German Shepherd develop a happy and healthy relationship.

In conclusion, training your German Shepherd is an important part of making sure that both you and your dog live healthy and happy lives. If you follow the key strategies and advice in this guide, you can successfully train your German Shepherd and form a strong bond with him or her for the rest of your life. Make a point to show restriction, consistent, and flexible in your technique, and reliably search for capable help if essential. With effort and dedication, you can raise a companion who is loving and well-behaved.

Final thoughts on raising a well-behaved German Shepherd

Raising a well-behaved German Shepherd requires time, effort, and perseverance. It is essential to comprehend that training is an ongoing process and that consistency is essential. By following the advice in this guide and adapting it to your dog's particular personality and needs, you can help your German Shepherd become a happy, healthy, and well-behaved companion.

One of the most crucial aspects of training your German Shepherd is establishing yourself as the pack leader. Dogs need to be led because they live in packs. If you take on the role of pack leader, you can earn the trust, respect, and obedience of your dog. In addition to being composed, self-assured, and assertive, this demands clear expectations and boundaries.

Another crucial piece of setting up your German Shepherd is socialization. To avoid fear and animosity, it is essential to expose your dog to a variety of people, places, and things from an early age. By gradually introducing new experiences and stimuli, you can boost your dog's confidence and prevent behavioral issues.

Regular exercise, feeding, and grooming can also result in a well-behaved German Shepherd. Your canine's general wellbeing and prosperity can be improved and disastrous ways of behaving forestalled by giving adequate physical and mental excitement. In addition, feeding your dog the right food and bathing and grooming him or her on a regular basis can keep him or her healthy and help you stay close to your dog.

Focusing on your dog's unique needs and personality is important, along with preparation and routine consideration. It is important to be adaptable and patient when meeting the needs of individual German Shepherds, as some may require more socialization, exercise, or attention than others.

To wrap things up, developing a respectful German Shepherd requires major areas of strength for a to the turn of events and prosperity of your pet. By investing time and effort in training and care, you can bond with your dog for the rest of your life.

Commitment, persistence, and consistency are required to raise a respectful German Shepherd. Even though the interaction might be difficult at times, what you get in the end is a friend who stays true to you and cares about you, which makes your life more enjoyable. When working with your German Shepherd, remember to always focus on providing positive reinforcement, forming a strong bond, and promptly addressing any behavioral issues.

It's basic to in like manner remember that German Shepherds prosper with mental and genuine energy. Ensure that there are numerous opportunities for exercise, training, and socialization to avoid boredom and destructive behavior. In addition, maintaining a regular eating and cooking schedule can ensure that your German Shepherd remains in top condition.

In conclusion, raising a well-behaved German Shepherd requires dedication, perseverance, and consistency. By beginning training early, establishing clear rules and boundaries, and employing positive reinforcement, you can ensure that your dog is well-behaved and well-adjusted.

It is fundamental for remember that each canine is particular and that what works for one canine may not work for another. Make it a point to seek the assistance of an experienced dog coach if you really need additional direction, and adapt your preparation strategies to the circumstances.

In addition, it is essential to provide your German Shepherd with a lot of physical activity, socialization, and mental stimulation to reduce the risk of behavior issues and prevent fatigue. Regular health checks and vaccinations for your pet can also help keep them healthy.

Last but not least, remember that your German Shepherd is a loyal, dependable companion who only wants to please you. Love them, be patient with them, and keep up with your training so you can build a strong bond with them.

In conclusion, raising a well-behaved German Shepherd requires proper training, regular exercise, socialization, and mental stimulation. With hard work and consistency, you can raise a healthy, happy companion who will be a joy to have in your life.

Made in United States
Troutdale, OR
09/03/2023